Work For A Living
And Still Be Free
To Live

Eileen McDargh

BookPartners, Inc.
Wilsonville, Oregon

Library of Congress Cataloging in Publication Data
McDargh, Eileen.
        How to work for a living and still be free to live.
        Bibliography: p.
        1. Work.   2. Work — Psychological aspects   3. Life skills
I. Title
HD 4904.M39   1985   306.36   85-1846
(Previously published by Reston Publishing, Inc., ISBN 0-8359-2934-
5, and by Loch Lomond Press, ISBN 0-9623190-0-7)
ISBN 1-885221-54-1

Printed in the United States of America

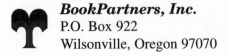 **BookPartners, Inc.**
P.O. Box 922
Wilsonville, Oregon 97070

To my treasured workmates, soulmates, and wombmates.

To be what we are, and to become what we are capable of becoming, is the only end of life.
-- *Robert Louis Stevenson*

Whatever you can do, or dream you can, begin it. Boldness has genius, power and magic in it.
– *Johann Wolfgang von Goethe*

Chaos trusted is a dancing star.
– *Friedrich Wilhelm Nietzsche*

Acknowledgments

With grateful appreciation, I am indebted to the many people who courageously shared their stories, feelings, and concerns with me. Whether anonymous or named, you provided my touchstone for reality.

My deepest thanks belong to my family, whose unconditional love and overwhelming support have always freed me to live. Thank you for encouraging me to be authentic rather than typecast and for taking up the slack when this book has called me away.

Contents

Priorities

We're working too hard
accomplishing a lot but …
the time to play is passing us by.

We're in our separate worlds
of creative concentration
It's wonderful but …
the time to be is passing us by.

We meet for meals
and speak of work
It's helpful but …
the time to know is passing us by.

We meet in bed
and go to sleep
It's restful but …
the time to love is passing us by.
                        – Natasha Josefowitz

Introduction

---

*Never for the sake of peace and quiet deny
your own feelings or experiences.*
– Dag Hammarskjold

Brilliantly said. Harder to do.

For many of us, the spinning circle of work, external pressures and internal agendas cram our twenty-four hours so full that we rarely take time to question why there's a sense of emptiness or loss of control in our lives. Or why we find ourselves getting up for work and saying "Good God, morning!" instead of "Good morning, God."

Consider this book your time out. And more.

If your day is partitioned into gray segments of work/eat/sleep—if you have to introduce yourself before having dinner with your children—if the business is running you instead of you running the business—if your soul hungers for a deeper meaning to life—you NEED more.

If your family and friends think you've flown over the cuckoo's nest when you wistfully talk about leaving your executive position for a country store in Snohomish, WA— if your last significant relationship was with your seventh-grade flame and you're too busy "working" to even remember his/her name—then there's a big hole in your todays that will dramatically impact your tomorrows.

Now here's the kicker: I wrote these words ten years ago. Sadly, they remain absolutely on target for today. In fact, even more so.

Consider the current evidence: Harvard economist Juliet Schor documents that Americans across all economic spectrums now put in an additional 163 hours (or one additional month) of work per year. Less than one in fifty Americans report any sense of balance. Downsized organizations have shed over 3.4 million workers at last count. Many of them have become entrepreneurs struggling to launch new businesses. For the survivors in shrinking firms, the workload didn't get smaller just because the workforce got smaller. A second shift of at-home labor begins after regular work hours. Meals have turned toward grazing. We now microwave everything and have lost the magic of the kitchen. Technology tracks us from boardrooms to bedrooms to bathrooms. We work everywhere.

Small wonder that the following books were on the best-seller list at the same time and also sold at Price Club and Sam's Club: *Beating the Street* by Wall Street guru Peter Lynch, and Thomas More's *Care of the Soul—How to Find Depth and Sacredness in Everyday Life.* These books mirror the essence of our common dilemma. How do we swim with the sharks, grow a business, earn a living and *still* claim lives of wholeness and quality? The evidence is mounting: for far too many of us, work seems to be working us. The packed agendas of our days result in life leading us rather than us leading a life. Now more than ever we seek to know how to work for a living and still be free to live.

Consider this your encouragement. You are not alone. There are, quite frankly, a lot of us in just such a spot, slugging it out in a vacuum and looking for something or someone to tell us "you're not crazy." It becomes apparent that just the simple sharing of experiences brings tremendous relief and support.

And so this is a lima bean book. It has grown from the seed of my work experiences and research into a supportive guide for individuals seeking balance within their careers and more to life than a paycheck. It has been fertilized by the candid life/work histories of teachers, corporate executives, entrepreneurs, medical professionals, engineers, athletes, artists, and others. And it has been warmed by an eagerness to relay a pattern for coming to terms with twenty-first-century business reality and personal needs.

What becomes patently clear is that the traditional model of balance as a pan-scale is fantasy—nothing is ever equal. We all are at different "phases" in our lives. We might be the newlyweds, the struggling parents, the caretaker for aging parents, the exhausted single parent, the high-flying, jump-starting career maker, the cancer-fighter, or the new-born baby tender. Each phase of our life requires different energies, different attentions.

Demands upon our time and energy will shift with the wind. In this book you will discover that I use sailing as a metaphor for balance. I'll help you personalize the five critical parts to our sailboat. The one constant, however, that we all share in our sailing through life, is the world of work.

Thus, for the greatest part of this book, the emphasis rests on exploring the business world.

Throughout the years as I have struggled to find my niche in the world of work, I've discovered numerous other professionals in a wide variety of fields and economic strata agonizing over the same questions: "Is this all there is to life?" "What do I *really* want to do?" From listening to their steps in handling such a dilemma and from comparing it to my experience, five things are now clear:

1. There are distinct stages to the process of answering these questions.
2. A new definition of "work" has emerged.
3. Honest personal evaluation is essential and probably the hardest task.
4. The essence of successful living is balance: a delicate juggling act of putting intellectual, material, physical, emotional and spiritual ingredients into our lives.
5. The working/living solutions of today will have to change as we grow and change. But if we understand the process (and how some other people handled it), hopefully the next phase won't be so overwhelming.

If only I had known these things way back when ... when life had as much gusto as stale beer ... when the corporate vice president accepted my resignation and said, "You're making a big mistake" ... when self-doubt and depression slapped my wrist. If only I had known there were others going through the same process ... that it *is* a *process*, a transactional unfolding of me which will be repeated again and again. If only....

I am writing this book to correct those "if onlys."

Because all of us must respond to the demands of life

in our own unique way, I'd like to think that this book contains a smorgasbord of ideas. Please take what appeals to you; leave the rest behind. I only ask that you allow yourself to mentally sample each section. Open yourself to the possibility that there just might be another mindset for approaching your work.

For this reason, you will find many choices in the book. Only choices. The answers must come from you. Some readers will find an affirmation, a giant "yes" to present or future plans. For others, perhaps a tap on the shoulder to move into action. And for the rest, perhaps a new perspective on a segment of the working population that transcends traditional labels, job descriptions and pigeon holes.

Some books are read with the mind. Others with the heart. This will require both.

Chapter One

This Thing Called "Work"

---- - ── - ── - ── - ── - ── - ── - ── - ── - ── - ──

My father taught me to work; he did not teach
me to like it.
— *Abe Lincoln*

I always admired dear old Abe. But when I found this
quote, I liked him even more. What could be better than
using a man of wisdom (and humor) to introduce a "must-
have" chapter.

Let's face it. We would be putting the cart before the
horse if we didn't first look at the big picture: changing
attitudes about work and ourselves as workers.

Do you remember bongo-thumping Maynard G.
Krebs in the '60s television comedy series *Dobie Gillis*? At
the mere mention of "work," Maynard's voice trembled,
rose an octave, and screeched in horror, "WORK!?!?" He
probably echoed a sentiment found in many of us. Small

wonder. Since the days when Adam and Eve left the Garden of Eden, labor traditionally has been coupled with groans and sweat. By medieval times, those workers and artisans who could put forth such effort but still take deep, satisfying pride in the product of their labors were to be envied. And as the Industrial Age moved workers further from intimate involvement in their work, personal satisfaction became an even rarer commodity.

By the 1900s, emphasis changed from the end result to the conditions under which humans worked. From the emergence of unions, to salary regulations, competitive and often elaborate benefit packages, computerization, and even psychologically designed office environments, we have attempted countless measures for making work more palatable. At the same time, and often at counter purposes, we've also tried to make it more productive.

But legislation, perks, mechanics and decor just weren't enough. Studs Terkel, in his 1972 classic book *Working,* found only a few individuals who relished their daily jobs. Non-recognition, the nature of the job, and humiliations from within and without were the chief complaints. Above all, he noted, "To survive the day is triumph enough for the walking wounded among the great many of us."

In the decades since Terkel's trek into the hidden corners of the American scene, the business world has attempted to change.

The buzzwords of re-engineering, empowerment, and self-managed teams float like mantras across many organizations. Trend-watcher John Naisbitt proclaims worker morale to be *the* issue of the nineties. Magazine article after magazine article bemoans the lack of energy, loyalty, and enthusiasm. We're told that morale equals motivation. So while managers look for ways to motivate employees, employees wait for the organizations to turn them on. Neither is doable.

Motivation is an inside-out job. Self-motivation is redundant. There is no other kind. The best that managers can do is to create an environment which improves the chances that employees will compel themselves to perform. This means that all of us have control over our own morale.

Imagine the sense of personal power if we could discover ways to control our response to our current job environment while freeing ourselves to make more authentic career decisions. Imagine the release we would feel if we could turn work fixation into fascination and make a reconnection with the rest of life.

Let's explore some current shifts in the workplace which will influence that flip from fixation into fascination.

Shift #1: A Move Away From Employment Guarantees.

The old social contract between companies and workers is dead and buried. Traditional notions of lifelong employment, guaranteed retirement, and clearly defined job ladders have faded into the sunset.

Cover after cover of business magazines speak about the demise of "the job."

Shifts like this often strike terror into hearts. After all, while this might not have been the job of our dreams, it was at least a paycheck. As with any life event, we have two choices: complain about the shift or create a personal game plan to deal with reality. Career resiliency and lack of job permanence can be an opportunity. No longer must you wait for some blessing from on high to develop skills, market yourself and take more responsibility for your own welfare.

Shift #2—A Move Toward Humanness

High technology continues to distance us from our work and from each other. As trend-watcher John Naisbitt points out, this high tech proficiency must be matched with even greater doses of high touch—massive quantities of human contact and caring.

Programs designed to help employees juggle the demands of their work and personal lives continue to grow in popularity. Childcare assistance grows with work/family programs offering everything from referral sources to on-site services. Acknowledging the aging boomer population, elder care is slowly being added to benefit programs along with flexible scheduling. Corporate sabbaticals are spreading. No longer the privilege of academics and senior executives, they're becoming a valuable tool.

Great. For a start. There's more to be done.

Opportunities for significant human interaction are limited within the job setting—particularly if the company depends upon software programs and inundations of paper to take the place of face-to-face communication. Additionally, workload often prohibits just how much time an individual can respond to external interactions with family, education, church, friends. Indeed there are still those firms who consider outside involvement to be a sign of weakness in employee ability.

Case in point: During a conversation, the president of a large consulting firm admitted privately that a job applicant was turned down because he was too involved with Little League and family affairs to put in the unspoken requisite of sixty hours per week. "And you know, Eileen," concluded the president, "I expect my employees to place company responsibilities first."

Now don't think that I'm discounting the reality that

employees frequently put in long hours. Goodness knows I can't even begin to count the days when I was the first one in a corporate office and one of the last to leave. But to make a conscious decision that work must *always* take precedence over other things in life is to deny a fully human existence.

Not only do we hunger for human contact within our jobs, but if living is our goal, we require time for the significant people in our lives *and* for ourselves. Getting a gold watch for putting in thirty years and sixty hours a week at the same company no longer holds wide appeal. We want more from both inside and outside our place of employment. In fact, a nationally recognized testing instrument used to assess the internal health of an organization now uses the amount of employee free time as one of the measures for a productive environment.

Shift #3 – A Move Toward Variety and Importance

Is your life the same now as it was ten years ago? Are you the same person you were ten years ago? How about five? Three? Maybe even yesterday? If you answered yes to the above, you either have been a victim of cryogenics or have been recently returned by some closely encountered group from Asteroid B-27.

Our lives are radically changed by the nanosecond-speed world we now inhabit. If anyone had told me ten years ago that I'd be writing with a computer, that my mail would come electronically, that corporate fitness experts would evolve from physical education teachers, that a computer would call me on the phone, that the Berlin Wall would fall and the Soviet Union shatter, that … that…. You name it.

-- .-- .-- .-- .-- .-- .-- .-- .-- .-- .-- .-- .-- .-- .-- .-- .-

And if I haven't experienced the change, at least I've read about it. The Information Age is upon us, telling us in detail often more than we care to know.

The implication for the world of work is that we are easily bored, stifled, and discontent with rigid environments. There is too much change around us for the static, the regimented, and—for many of us—the unimportant. We want to count, to have it matter that somewhere in a picture that's larger than ourselves, our life is significant.

These shifts, I think, account for the fact that we often feel like we're in a tailspin, wanting more in our lives than just punching a clock.

It has been said that we fear not death, but death with insignificance. The biggest shift in the American workforce is a yearning for meaning in what we do. Terkel concludes that "most of us have jobs that are too small for our spirits."

> We work to become, not to acquire
> *– Elbert Hubbard*

Let's Throw Webster
Out the Window

With these shifts, I think we need to redefine just what work is and is not.

Let's start with the obvious. An old Irish proverb defines work as "the yeast that raises dough." Granted, some of us might end up with massive loaves and others with pita bread, but earning money is certainly a real portion to our definition.

At first glance, the tendency is to place primary emphasis on this definition: "Work is what one gets paid for." Why else would more women now be employed outside the home than at any previous time in our history?

Right???

Wrong. According to a *New York Times* poll, the majority of American women believe that their place is on the job; that work and independence are elements of life as satisfying as spouses, homes and children. In fact, even if they could afford it, 58 percent of U.S. working women said they would rather work than stay at home.

There must be something *more* to work than pay.

Jean Paul Sartre, the Nobel award-winning author, struck mental gold when he claimed that work was "the significance of an individual."

Check it out at any cocktail party. The conversation will probably go like this:

"Hi, my name is John. I'm a neighbor of Pete and Jan's. I saw you standing by the chopped liver and thought I'd come over and get acquainted."

"Er, my name is Eileen." (If it's me, I'm mumbling through a mouthful of pâté and cracker.)

"Well, what do you do?"

There you have it. My significance, my identity is now coming from the work that I do. What dear John is REALLY asking is, "Who are you?" It's not that he's being sly or circumspect. After all, if he did ask me who I was, chances are I'd reply with, "I'm a management consultant and a speaker." Even I define myself in such terms.

Still doubt the power of work to give us identity?

Imagine you are unemployed and cocktail-party John asks that question. Would a hot flush zoom up your neck as you reply, "I'm currently exploring alternatives?" Would you cross your fingers and state, "I'm independently wealthy?"

One in-between-jobs executive told me that she felt

worthless and small when confronted with such questions.

A business editor who had just been notified of his publication's demise, responded even more strongly. "I'm now a nobody. As an editor I had clout. Could get in anywhere; talk with anyone. Who's going to give the time of day to just untitled me?"

For these people, for many of us, work even has power over our self-esteem and our personal sense of who we are!

In his landmark book, *Work and Love: The Crucial Balance,* Dr. Jay B. Rohrlich confirms this fact:

"There are many kinds of self symbols: feelings, interests, loves, memories, opinions, tastes, clothing styles, national heritages, religions, material posses- sions, memberships, etc. But to give uniqueness to an individual, one relies most fully on one's 'piece of work.' All other associations are more passive expressions of self than what we do."

Unfortunately, too often we select work because the title has character and immediate recognition. But is that job, that title, what really brings out our true sense of self? Now more than ever, Sartre's explanation is a valid part in our new "work" definition.

I think a blend of both is the answer. The definition I prefer came from a sprightly woman with over seventy years of living and learning to her credit: "A job is what you do for money. Work is what you do for a life."

Ahh. What insight!

She continued, "'Work' is what energizes, gives meaning and significance to the very unique talents we all possess. Life then becomes the balance of all those essential physical, emotional, material, mental, and spiritual compo- nents that create a life worth truly living."

I got the message.

Here's Our New Definition

To rephrase my dear septuagenarian: Work is that significant, energizing activity which provides meaning to life. It is not necessarily the source of livelihood, but it is, most assuredly, that which makes you alive.

You have a special talent, a unique gift, a definite role to play on Planet Earth which is yours and yours alone. Whether you've reached the place on Life's stage in which it is time to move into an entirely different role for Act II or even Act III, or you're standing in the wings auditioning for a part, you are gifted.

In simple terms, your gift—what I consider to be your *real* work—is that energizing activity during which time melts away as you become absorbed in the "doing." You burn on all four burners and despite probable challenges, there is a sense of accomplishment, passion, and purpose. It might be as straightforward as shelving books at the library or as complex as writing software programs to monitor trajectory patterns for space vehicles. As Barbara Sher, author of *Wishcraft,* insists, it means "getting what you want. Not what your father or mother wanted for you, not what you think you can realistically get in this world, but what you want."

Think of the implications within this definition: Many of us might have "jobs" but no work! Imagine what energizes, challenges, and excites you. Why, it might be any number of things from the most complex down to the simplest: designing software, singing, gardening, counseling, working with tools, telling children's stories, exploring new cities, selling a product, balancing ledger sheets, baking cookies, saving souls.

Is your energizing "work" part of your job? Do you even know what that "work" is? Is your life so out of balance that you wouldn't know "work" from "job" if it whistled Yankee Doodle?

Whatever it is, the role of this book is to give you support and permission (which ultimately you must give to yourself) to make choices which will put your life in balance and allow you to live and "work" at the same time.

But it's not easy. The not-free-to-live feeling comes as a result of one or more of the following:

1. We are spending so much time at our "job" that there is nothing left for our "work" as well as our personal life.
2. We are spending so much energy at our "work" that other vital life components are out of balance.
3. We don't know what our "work" is.
4. We don't know (or won't accept) that we can live in balance and harmony.
5. We are afraid to risk and change.
6. We are afraid of the future.
7. We set limits on ourselves.
8. We see ourselves as powerless.

In the long run, the ultimate task is to make "job" and "work" synonymous. Even that's not an easy chore. For one thing, most of us don't consider such mingling to be possible.

During my first year as a consultant, I found myself accepting public relations clients seeking publicity. Although I had well-established credentials and could easily handle the assignments, something was wrong.

Ah hah! I soon realized that the reason I started out on my own was *not* to start a public relations agency, but to handle communication problems which I found more meaningful: training in interpersonal skills; analyzing and developing a smooth communication flow between management and employees; speaking. I felt no energy in getting someone's face on prime-time television.

Suddenly I knew why I kept turning down some clients, accepting others; doubting one day and believing the next; receiving conflicting feelings from my stomach and my heart. Instinctively, I was aiming at my "work" and not a job. But the bank balance and old mental tapes were pushing me into accepting "jobs" instead of concentrating on my "work."

I'm still struggling. But along the way have come some insights about this process of "working" and "living." For example, I now know we might have to accept a "job" until such times as we can do our "work." Or, we might keep a "job" in order to support our "work." I can readily see that our choice of everything from material possessions to physical exercise impacts the balance and calm surrounding either "work" or a "job."

But I also have learned that we have absolute freedom (and therefore responsibility) to choose what goes into our life *and* to choose how we feel about that life.

The problem is that frequently we don't know what powerful choices we have. In fact, we might not even wish to examine our lives because we see ourselves as formed in concrete and without opportunity for change.

It seems hidden attitudes get in the way.

Some Stumbling Blocks to Working and Living

No matter how old we are, we carry attitudes with us: attitudes about ourselves, work, other people, and the world in general. Not all attitudes are healthy. Some might keep us from really growing, changing, and deeply living. Since our current employment is where we concentrate at least one half of our waking time, it stands to reason that these attitudes will probably be expressed within our job. Some of these attitudes, attached to us with mental superglue, can prevent us from honestly looking at our present work. Just as soon as we start to question where we are—zap—the attitude becomes a Star Trek force field that throws us back into inaction.

Sit back now and reflect if you might possibly be holding any of these attitudes. If you are, for the time being, merely acknowledge that fact.

Attitude One: I Cannot Waste What I Was Educated to Do

Amazing what a piece of sheepskin can do to promote immobility. Not surprising, though. Most of us worked extremely hard, at great financial risk, to gain the educational objective we fixed our star upon when we were in our late teens and early twenties.

Why did we choose what we did? Robert Wendorf, a psychotherapist, received this very clear message from his Russian immigrant parents. "I think I was five when I heard my mother introduce me to her friends as, 'This is Robert. He'll be a doctor.' My uncle was a physician and, to my parents, wherever God was, Uncle Zeke was four steps above Him. I grew up on stories of Uncle Z. struggling through the snow in winter to become a doctor; paying back my grandparents by cleaning spittoons. It was very much a matter of success *and* paying back my parents for whatever they sacrificed. When I told Mama I didn't want to be a doctor, she looked at Grandmama, shrugged her shoulders and said, 'Well, you must follow your heart—so you'll be a dentist.'"

It's funny now when Robert tells the story. But little humor came with the original message—without those careers, Robert would never make it.

"Making it" seemed to play a heavy role in the majority of academic decisions. Which professions earned substantial incomes. Which professions would be in demand at graduation. Which professions would bring a beaming nod of approval from our societal and/or familial group, influenced—and still do—the choice of higher degrees.

And probably, for many of us, we did hit upon something that we liked to do ... *at that time in our lives.*

Having taught school and been guilty of asking students what they will be when they grow up, I can only beg for mercy and plead temporary insanity for asking that question. After personal trial and error, let the truth be known: I'm going to be lots of things when I grow up! (And I'm not finished growing.)

Doesn't that make better sense? You are *not* the same person today as you were fifteen years ago. Perhaps you've uncovered new talents, other interests, and your college education seems only mildly relative to what you'd really like to do.

The higher the education, the harder it will be to

overturn this attitude. Ronda S., a speech therapist whose story you will encounter later, acknowledged that for some time she kept ignoring thoughts of discontent and change because "I was already trained. What else did I know how to do? Why, I figured it would be crazy to throw away what I had learned."

Even if you succeed in convincing yourself to explore alternatives, society seems to have a hard time with it. "After I took a leave of absence from the school and began to explore other possibilities, more often than not, prospective employers would look at me in disbelief and ask why I was doing something as foolish as considering leaving my profession!" recalled Ronda.

The NASA engineer-turned-artist, the chemist-turned-management consultant, the ophthalmologist-turned-novelist are but a scattering of the people I've interviewed who had to acknowledge and change such an attitude in order to put true work and balance in their lives.

Attitude Two: To Be a Success, I Must Make a Lot of Money

Once upon a time it was enough to have a chicken in every pot. Now, you better add VCRs, home computers, designer jeans, and food processors. Yep—it all takes money. The problem is, the money begins to control us rather than the other way around.

In one sense, our attitude toward money might be part of our nation's inheritance. The Calvinist work ethic not only urged our founding fathers to put their noses to the grindstone, but also proclaimed financial bounty as a "blessing" from the Most High.

Some of this attitude might also have come from personal or parental experience with the Great Depression. Never before in the history of our nation had survival been such an issue. What money could buy was critical.

Is there any wonder that the deep recessions of the last twenty years may have triggered a nightmare memory for many people? Or if we don't remember the Depression, there are those who call it to mind.

During the 1980-81 recession, whenever I called my mother long distance, she inevitably ended the conversation with this warning: "Don't call me. Save your money. You'll never know when this will get worse." It's hard not to have that ghost-of-bad-times-past rub off and to become fearful about one's future solvency.

Unfortunately, rather than needing money for survival, I have found it more common that money is needed for "things." Or at least to give the impression of "things." I'd be willing to bet my one diamond ring that we all know a business-woman (or man) who drives a Mercedes convertible, wears designer clothes, insists on first-class airline seats, and lives in *the* exclusive residential community. However, get them in conversation and you'll find they live in fear: afraid that something will happen to the growing business. Why, they might lose the Mercedes! Or the estate! But ... in the process of the job (or maybe even "work"), they have also lost contact with children, the spouse is but a distant memory, and there are no close friends. Feeding the lifestyle dragon created tremendous imbalance. Simple question: Is this success? Is this living? Was it worth it?

According to New York clinical psychologist Dr. Jeffrey Blum, money just doesn't buy happiness. Based upon his personal experience and also his work as a

therapist in community clinics and posh psychiatric facili-
ties for the very affluent, he reached this conclusion about
money: "More than anything else, money resembles
cocaine. You can never have enough; you need more to get
the same high; it leaves you depressed and it is overrated."

The problem comes when making money, rather than
making a life, becomes the single reason for hopping out of
bed in the morning.

Attitude Three: Money is the Root of All Evil and I'll Be a Bad Person If I Make Too Much

Here's the flip side of Attitude Two. It's one that can
be just as damaging and keep us from honestly looking at
our work and the thing we call "living."

Those of us who didn't get the Calvinist message
heard another one. Namely, it is easier for a camel to waddle
through the needle's eye than for a rich person to find
heavenly happiness. Then too, let's not forget the all-too-
human trait of disparaging those who have what we would
really like. If we came from a family that perceived itself to
be on the lower economic rung, the eternal antagonism
between the haves and the have-nots might be a constant
refrain that haunts our subconscious.

To make matters worse, quite a few of us decided that
we weren't doing enough to deserve more money; that we'd
look greedy and selfish if we asked for more; that if we
were in a service position like social work or teaching, the
benefits should be heartfelt and not pocketfelt.

Personally, it has taken me quite some time to
acknowledge that it is okay to be substantially paid for

what I do; that money, kept in its proper perspective, is okay and—as the commercial says—I'm worth it! Now, the criteria for how much work and how much money is directly related to the way in which I define the value and quality of my service. But until I realized that I was influenced by such an attitude, I was not honestly looking at my work/life.

Attitudes Two and Three seem to cause the most hangups in examining not only our current work/job, but also in determining our future actions. But we'll talk more about money later.

Attitude Four: If I Make A Mistake, I'm No Good

Looking at where you are in life and where you are going is risky business. After all, the mirror on the wall might call for change. There's something warm and easy about staying exactly where you are in life. Don't rattle the cage. Put more layers of mental insulation around your feelings. Stay safe because what if you make a move and— horrors!—you make a mistake. You were wrong. You were better off where you were.

Granted, choices which dramatically impact others must be made with moral and ethical considerations. One doesn't just close down a manufacturing plant, fire employees and run to Bora Bora because life needs a change. Nor does one place the family fortune on Gallant Steed to place in the third, lose, and walk away saying, "Oh well, such is life." These choices can be big, big mistakes.

However, when the above attitude is one that prevents personal growth, it's a sure-fire guarantee that juices will dry up and you'll turn into a dull, prune-souled individual. If you take nothing more from this book, at least allow yourself to recognize the harm in holding such an attitude about yourself close to your fearful heart.

In fact, I like the mindset of a gutsy woman writer in her late forties who came to Hollywood with about $1,500 in her pocket, a teenage daughter, and only the vague inclination of a potential job. When challenged by well-meaning friends about this very obvious wrong move, she'd retort, "There's no such thing as mistakes ... only choices from which we learn, grow, and advance."

She was convinced, despite the gloomy predictions of friends, that it was *not* a mistake to seek a job that could become her "work." It was a choice—not a mistake. And, I'm happy to report, after six years and seeing her daughter through high school, Sunny F. is making a go of her true work.

What a tremendous release if we could relinquish the fear of making a wrong move, a mistake, and instead adopt the mindset that chants, "I am making a choice for growth." No matter how that choice turns out, I am convinced of the tremendous benefit.

Try It For Yourself

Take a personal incident which you now consider a "mistake" and imagine what it would be like if it had not occurred.

To do this, you might find it beneficial to try a stream-of-consciousness form of free-flow writing. Sit wherever you are most comfortable, with pencil and notebook on your lap. Now, taking deep breaths from the pit of your stomach, allow yourself to relax.

When you feel ready, let yourself write—without censorship—whatever comes up for you as you ask yourself, "What would my life be like now if I had not _____?

Write out that scenario and how you feel about it. Make sure you note what persons, things, events, and insights would no longer be present in this "new" choice.

I am confident that you will then release yourself from the fear of personal loss through mistakes—because such choices ultimately bring benefit with them. Besides, some choices just have to be tried. What is worse than not succeeding is to spend the rest of your life wondering if you should have made a certain move and wishing you had.

I used this method of free-flow writing as a means to get some insight into what would often be called a "mistake"—a marriage that ended in divorce. What I discovered was how much that marriage brought into my life, how much I learned about myself, how many wonderful, significant people are now in my life, even how a new profession and life blossomed *because* of that so-called "mistake." Yes, I'd do it all again, pain and all. Tremendous good bubbled over.

Great discoveries have also come from so-called mistakes. Some of our wonders of modern science have come because someone made an error, did something that was wrong. What do you know? Voila! A new enzyme. A new cure. A breakthrough.

I encourage you to allow yourself such a breakthrough. Take a respite and ask yourself if any of these attitudes might prohibit you from looking more deeply into your "work," job and life.

As you continue to read the following chapters, become conscious if any of these attitudes begin to wave a

--·--

warning flag. Listen and see if an attitude talks to you,
trying to convince you that you couldn't possibly make
such choices. Maybe you hear the voice of a parent or a
relative.

Then ask yourself if you wish to listen to that voice or
attempt to risk. The most important voice to hear is your
own. It might be the one which hasn't gotten a word in
edgewise for years.

This is all well and good but....

What if you feel too hopeless or helpless where you
are right now to even consider a change?

What if you've made too many changes, only to find
that the euphoric honeymoon of each new job gets shorter
and shorter?

What if current financial demands seem to require that
you stay put in a place where you feel put upon?

What if your organization is one of the many which
has flattened out the pyramid for upward mobility—the
only immediate key you see to salvation?

What if you are in the place where you have always
wanted to be but find yourself inundated with the same
problems you thought you had left behind?

What if you don't really know what you want and find
yourself saying, "Hey, what can you expect? It's a job."

Does this mean that once again you must postpone
happiness while waiting for the company to change, the
boss to be transferred, the perfect work choice to be made,
the proverbial ship to come in, the rules to be altered, the
work load to be lessened, or the highest degree to be
conferred?

No. No. No.

We do terrible mischief to ourselves by not learning
how to flow with our current work experience rather than

fight it or flee from it as our first recourse. To explain a little further, assume that your "gift," your dream work, is sitting on a rock ten miles downstream from a terrible stretch of white water. If you've ever run a river, you know that moving outside the tongue of the water (which looks as if it is attached to the very throat of the rapids) can very likely smash your craft against boulders. Portage around the boiling spot can throw you into dense thickets and impassable rock walls and is only considered as a final measure. You don't wait for some thundercloud to flood the river and raise the water table. Instead you deliberately, powerfully, steer into the rough water and after a few seconds' soaking, emerge at the end into a calm stream.

So too in your life. You mustn't wait. You'll make better, faster, more authentic progress to your dreams if you move from a sense of power and personal control over where you are right now! You might even find that you ARE in the right place to begin with.

The purpose of this book is to provide immediate help for today, wherever you find yourself. Using real life examples, exercises, and researched methods, you'll discover ways to transform the ordinary into the extraordinary, to take charge of your response to the job environment—in short, to make work "work" for you AND to create a daily program for remaining connected to the rest of your life.

Self-mastery of what is generates the fuel to move toward what can be.

There is one small thing which can stand in the way of being able to master and move from what "is" to what "can be"—the napping mind. Think about it this way:

You're driving down a road when all at once you realize that you have gone beyond your destination. Your mind was off on another channel and you have simply been going through the motions of driving. Startled, you look around, get your bearings, and try to figure out an alternative route. (You might also blame a passenger for distracting you.) What a frightening experience when you realize how much mechanical power was in your hands while you were oblivious to what was going on.

The same thing is true in our everyday lives. We move in and out of consciousness, unaware of the power we hold to alter our course. Too often, it's a traumatic event which snaps us into the here and now. May I suggest that you take your time with this book and fine tune your mental antennae to who you are, what you're presently doing, how you're behaving, and what might be done differently to allow you to live this day, stop blaming the passenger, and get on with the higher task of finding and becoming who you really want to be.

Lastly, in order to re-examine, reclaim, renew, and rejoice with this new-found sense of control in your work, remember the words of Sam Keen: "If what you see is what you get, then first you must change your eyes."

Let us look together at our work.

Some Recommendations For Reading

I've arranged the following chapters according to the steps of the work/life evaluation process which appear to unfold in our lives. The word "steps" is important. Although some might occur simultaneously or possibly with years in between, to skip a step seems to result in imbalance. For example, we've first got to recognize what are our symptoms of discontent. We must explore our talents, needs, and feelings before we can make decisions to act on potential solutions. We must determine what "living" means to us so that our "job" or "work" choices are compatible. And once a choice is made, it is wise to know what to expect in the way of ups and downs, risks and rewards.

Let's begin that deeper look.

Summary

1. A "job" is what you do for a paycheck. "Work" is what you do for a life.
2. Work is that significant, energizing activity which provides meaning to life. The ultimate task is to make "work" and "job" synonymous.
3. You might have to accept a "job" until you find your "work." You might keep a "job" to support your "work." But at all times, balance is the key to really living.
4. We have absolute control over everything in our lives because we have the power to choose. We choose our attitudes, how we feel about our "job," how we define "living." We can choose to strive for balance. We can choose to fully live.
5. Some attitudes that might hinder us from honestly looking at our work or job are:
   - I cannot waste what I was educated to do.
   - To be a success, I must make a lot of money.
   - To be a good person, I can't make too much money because money is evil.
   - I'm no good if I make a mistake.
6. Most decisions are not "mistakes" but rather choices for growth.
7. If you are not in a place to "change," consider actions which can lead to feeling in control.

The great tragedy of our lives is that the major question of our existence is never put BY us—it is put by personal and social impulsiveness FOR us. Especially is this true in today's materialist, objectifying, authoritarian society, which couldn't care less about a person answering for himself the main question of life: "What is my unique gift, my authentic talent?"

As the great Carlyle saw, this is the main problem of a life, the only genuine problem, the one that should bother and preoccupy us all through the early years of our struggle for identity; all through the early years when we are tempted to solve the problem of our identity by taking the expedient that our parents, the corporation, the nation offer us; and it is the one that does bother many of us in middle and later years when we pass everything in review to see if we really had discovered it when we thought we did.

The way things are set up we are rewarded, so to speak, for NOT finding our authentic talent. The result is that most of our life is in large part a rationalization of our failure to find out who we really are, what our basic strength is, what thing it is that we were meant to work upon the world. The question of what one's talent is must always be related to how he works it on the world.

> — E. Becker, *The Birth and Death of Meaning*
> *(New York: Free Press—paperback,*
> *1971)*

Chapter Two

When You're Stuck In the Mud

——·——·——·——·——·——·——·——·——·——

How to turn from Frog to Prince (or Princess)
"Krrribitt"

You wouldn't have picked up this book unless you were in a situation which seemed to be getting the better of you. You might be looking at alternatives, but somehow all your mental ability seems to be caught up thrashing over the work setting in which you find yourself. You need some answers, or at least some clues, as to why others seem to be enjoying and thriving in their occupations while you are feeling frustrated, maybe angry, bored, fatigued, unmotivated and spending energy getting nowhere.

"It's not fair," you mutter to yourself. "I just need a break like those other folks...."

"If only this company were larger (or smaller)...."

"If my job description were different...."

"If there were only more excitement and challenge in what I am doing...."

"If I could just have that one bread-and-butter client...."

"If the company would appreciate the hard work I do...."

"If only there wasn't so much paperwork and so many meetings...."

"If I didn't have to deal with so many unreasonable people...."

"If the kids were through college and I could go out on my own...."

"If I were paid more money...."

And on and on goes the internal, infernal chatter which seems to merely stress just how much you need to be someplace else and someone else.

After all, those folks who appear to enjoy their work pretty much all the time must be blessed with the ideal job. It is as if, by magic, the Wizard of Id had waved his star-spangled wand and transformed those wart-covered positions into tasks fit for royalty and, in the process, changed them from feeling like hop toads into members of the royal family.

And in a way, the analogy is correct. Except that the magic is not in the nature of the work but rather in the worker. They are wizards in their own right, capable of transforming coal into diamonds—for diamonds are nothing more than black lumps which stuck to their business under pressure.

That's not to say these magicians aren't making tracks for moving into other arenas...for finding that dream work which represents their special gift and talent. However, by learning how to take control and respond positively to whatever the job situation dishes out, they have energy left over to stretch, grow, risk, and glow.

To give you an idea as to how differently a prince (princess) and a frog operate in the world of the gainfully employed, let's look at some real-life examples.

I think we begin to get a picture of ourselves when we start to identify with others. For this reason, I have paired the case studies as closely as possible to their occupations. Discover how each one responds to what is currently going on in the work environment. See if you can identify what parts within the job description seem, at face value, to create the frog factor.

Also note your reactions when you first think of each person's line of work. Consider just how much excitement, reward, recognition, income, and satisfaction we stereotypically assign to that job title—all qualities which we arbitrarily think of as the "ideal" job.

And here's our cast:

Steve Mitchell, door-to-door sales representative of cleaning products, who literally walked into my life.

It was about six-thirty one evening when the door to my office opened and a merry voice hollered out, "I'm here to solve your cleaning problems!"

Startled, I raced to the reception desk, only to find a thin young man with a squirt bottle, rag, and a grin that wrapped around his face like the grille of a 1975 Camaro.

"That's right. This is the product you've been waiting for. My name is Stevie ... now just watch."

Too amused to disobey, I watched in amazement

as he raced from carpet to wall to window, squirting and wiping, squirting and wiping.

"Now, isn't that something. It's non-toxic." (He opened the bottle and drank some of the fluid.) "And it's odorless." (He stuck the bottle under my nose.)

Interested, I began asking him questions—not only about the product but, more importantly, about himself. No, this wasn't his dream job. He had a degree in broadcasting from Temple University in Philadelphia. His real love was radio and the life of a disc jockey. Gab was his gift.

"I'm going to own a radio station one day. It costs $1.5 million, and this job is going to help me get it. Next month, I'll cut back on the time and begin to rep labels from musicians. But these four years have led me from Philadelphia to Los Angeles. No ma'am, it's been good."

With that, he tapped out a beat on the counter of the secretary's desk and began jiving out a jingle about dirt, spots, and his product.

"Don't tell me they taught you that song, too?"

"Oh no, ma'am. That was my way to keep from getting bored when I learned all the spots this stuff worked on."

He left with money is his pocket.

⚜

George S. (fictitious name), a postal carrier in a small, historic business community.

The new tenant of an upstairs office in a two-story building couldn't figure out why his mail had not been picked up in a week. After all, he had seen the postal truck in the parking lot, but no carrier.

Then one day, while talking with the occupants

of another office, postal clerk George walked in. A tall, well-proportioned man probably in his late twenties, George just stared at the newcomer, who introduced himself and asked about mail delivery.

"I hate having to walk up stairs," George grumbled. "Do you see all the buildings on this route?"

The newcomer glanced down the street at the single- and two-story buildings now restored to the days of Spanish simplicity and balconied charm. "Aren't you glad this isn't New York!"

"Well, how would you like to deliver this stuff?" The carrier waved an advertisement tabloid. "This is just junk."

"I don't care what you think is junk. I want my mail delivered and picked up like everybody else."

The carrier shrugged his shoulders, pushed his wire-rimmed glasses back on his nose, and left.

"What a miserable character," commented the tenant.

꧁꧂

Question: Is there any problem picking out the frog from the prince? Stevie sees possibilities, takes charge for turning routine into fun. George views the primary task of being a mail carrier as a burden. Interestingly enough, George has held his job for quite some time with misery as company.

꧁꧂

Ives R. (fictitious name), head of licensing for a multi-million-dollar entertainment conglomerate.

Clouds of smoke part like the Red Sea when entering Ives' office. T-shirts, stuffed animals, toys, and games are scattered around the room—remnants of a job well done in turning a film character into marketable products.

Ives breathes a sigh. "Well, I'm as happy as I could be working. There's just too much to do. I'm surrounded by incompetent people. And I get sick of haggling over the numbers with potential vendors. But, they pay me too much money to leave."

Harry M. (fictitious name), chief executive of a prominent shopping center development company

At age sixty-two, two books of poetry under his belt and a list of civic commitments which would tax the energy of a pint-sized atomic bomb, Harry's eyes sparkle when he talks about his four children, his wife, the art world, and his upcoming shopping center projects.

"We've taken this one mall and turned it into a focal point for the community with an amazing array of customer services: uniformed hostesses to answer shoppers' questions, pet-sitting services, free wheelchairs, specially designed baby strollers and free baby-sitting services. We look at each new project as a chance to be creative."

He admits that it's not easy. Dealing with city officials, community concerns, a fluctuating economy, and lawyers are part of the necessary headaches.

"But I even relish that. I look at each interaction as an opportunity to learn something about the other person, to see how creative I can be so that everybody wins in the process. Sure I get frustrated. But that's all part of the territory."

❧

Question: How do frogs and princes view their interactions with other people? Who takes lemons and makes lemonade?

❧

In 1981, career guru Richard Bolles read a story about a checker in a supermarket and later shared the tale in his newsletter. Although much time has passed, this princess's magic still carries a vivid example of alchemy at work.

Barbara (fictitious name), supermarket checker
"It's a job that few people would enjoy even a fraction of the time, and yet supermarket checker Barbara has "transformed the act of making the turntable start the food toward her: she does a little two-step, during which she causes her hips to hit the little bar that moves the turntable.

'Just wiggle your hips and the stuff keeps coming at you,' she says laughing.

She has transformed the picking up of the cans and things: she tries to see how fast she can make them move. She has transformed the racking up of the merchandise on the cash register: she gets a rhythm going, much like a musician would. She has transformed the bagging of the merchandise: she sees it as a puzzle, trying to fit the pieces the best way possible within the bag. She has also trans-formed the dealing with the customers: she notes those with lonely faces, admires something they have on or otherwise fusses over them a little. She notes the children and brings in cookies she has baked at home to share with them when they come through her line. She responds in different ways to each customer, reserving her warmest response for the 'customer who treats me like a human being, not like a robot back here.'

She is given a job as a checker, but she becomes a dancer, a racer, a musician, a puzzle-solver, a counselor and a Santa Claus. A fifty-six-year-old one, at that."

Pretty powerful picture. Particularly when contrasted with a checker I observed last week while standing in line. The checker said not a word to customers except "paper or plastic bags." An elderly customer, her wrist wrapped in an Ace bandage, struggled to lift the items from her cart to the counter. Rolling his eyes heavenward, the clerk folded his arms, gave a how-can-you-be-so-slow sigh, and made no move to help.

Sure, the customer behind the woman quickly moved to her aid and the clerk proceeded—without comment—to ring up the groceries. But the checker's obvious job unhappiness sent a blast of cold air down the line.

❧

Question: Who controls responses to the situation? Do frogs or princesses think in terms of other people? Who likes to turn work into play?

❧

Bill no-last-name, the cook for a rescue mission in the Southern California desert.

On Thanksgiving Day, the line around the mission bulged like the proverbial python, stuffed with humanity dressed in everything from unwashed rags to the humble dignity of a coat two sizes too small and a spotted tie for the holiday occasion.

Inside, Bill, a wiry little man—Popeye's double in starched whites—heaved a cauldron of giblet gravy to the back gas burner. He grinned at the volunteers, showing red gums around his two remaining teeth.

"Tell 'em they can come in now. We're ready to start dishing it out."

Amazingly, the small kitchen with its dented pots and pans and borrowed utensils spewed out ample food that day for some four hundred folks, while Bill presided over the scene like a benevolent gnome. He'd been up for two days, cooking turkeys, making stuffing, cutting potatoes, and baking pies. Yet on "The Day," all traces of chaos had vanished.

"You see, there's a secret to all of this. You just have to plan ahead, be orderly, take it one step at a time, and it all fits in." He paused to banter a call from one of the mission regulars.

"I cooked in the Navy" (no wonder he looked like Popeye!) "and always thought I'd like to try it full time. 'Sides, it's regular and I've got control of this little space. It's mine. 'Sides, they *like* my cooking."

⚜

Susan R. (fictitious name), accountant for a community clinic.

To enter Susan's office, one treads carefully. Stacks of invoices cover her desk and file folders are thrown around in disarray. The remnants of yesterday's lunch break are on a file cabinet and miscellaneous paper piles occupy other parts of the floor space.

"I just can't tell you how much work I am expected to do. It's driving me crazy." She puts her head in her hands and begins to cry.

"I feel so uptight about all of this. I'm also supposed to write policy on money procedures and yet I can't get the paperwork done. Nobody understands how hard I work. It's so hopeless."

Question: Who begins to control the environment? Who takes control one step at a time?

Jane H., president of a customer service research and training organization.

Her soft accent breaking through the noise of the luncheon meeting, Jane talks with pride about her company.

"We have three hundred 'mystery shoppers' who work for us, and they do such a super job. That's what customer service is all about anyway—treating people like you'd want to be treated. We work with our employees, train them, and help them perform. I have the best partner and people to work with. We just take care of each other and do good work."

She paused for a minute and added in a whisper, "Why, we're looking at doing one million in business this year."

Priscilla P. (composite), president and owner of a prominent advertising firm.

She sips her Perrier and shakes her head. "Good help is so hard to find. You think you've found someone and bingo! He makes mistakes; she wants to go home at five o'clock or else I'm just not sure that I can trust them."

She admits to having a temper but insists that it is necessary when her name is attached to the business.

"And can you imagine this?" She leans forward and whispers. "the other day, one of my account executives and I were in a meeting and my employee yawned! Right there—in front of the client. That's just not acceptable!"

꧁

Question: How does real royalty regard their subjects? Who sees human beings as potentially positive or potentially dangerous? Who lives the more peaceful life?

What Does It All Mean?

Standing aside and looking at the actions of others often gives us a pretty good insight into just what 'they" are doing wrong. It's certainly easier to see the freckle on someone else's cheek than the wart on our own nose. But hopefully, seeing the freckle, we're tempted to run to a mirror, peer carefully at ourselves, and see if there might be something there which we hadn't noticed before.

Or sometimes, if the freckle looks suspiciously similar to one we have, there is a temptation to wave it aside, make excuses, or discount it entirely.

Please don't. The ability to take control over wherever you find yourself in the world of work requires honest, candid personal evaluation. It means critically looking at the activating agent which seems to push those out-of-control, miserable buttons. Then, and only then, can you begin to assess *what* might be done to alter the results you're experiencing.

But the first step is locating the activating agent. Once you've isolated just what keeps work from working for you, you can begin a process of determining just what you can do to get control back.

Let's be honest. The chance of finding your perfect work—with *everything* exactly as you want it—has about the same odds as you finding another Hope diamond. What makes the difference between the frog and the prince is how much attention each pays to the not-so-wonderful aspects of work. It reminds me of the old rhyme: "Two men looked out from prison bars. One saw mud. The other saw stars."

Did you also notice that the job description, title, and imagined salary of the various case studies didn't seem to make a difference in whether or not someone was happy. What made the difference was how each chose to respond to the situation.

Activating Agents: The Potion Which Makes a Frog or Prince(ess)

If you are going to gain some control back in your life and handle the reality around you, then it is necessary to get a clear picture on exactly what you respond to (and how) which keeps the job or the work from working for you.

At this stage, we're not concerned about whether the activating agent has the force of a major hurricane or a weak tropical disturbance. Besides, as long as it is significant to you, it IS big. Later on, when you've regained some control, you might discover that the hurricane is diminished to a spring shower.

In the following section, see if you can identify what seems true for you. The lines after the questions are there *in case* you would like to jot down some thoughts which come to mind. Often, putting things in writing begins to clarify issues and areas for us.

Activating Agent #1:
Going Through the Motions

The words that best describe this category are: routine, little challenge, repetitive tasks, no sense of accomplishment, boredom, no sense of purpose or meaning.

The reality is that all tasks, no matter how exciting they are in the beginning, have a way of becoming routine. Don't we all know some people in glamour jobs and when we oooh and ahhh about what they do, they look at us blankly. What seems so marvelous to us has become as exciting as day-old socks for them.

I think the greater heroes are those folks, like the dancing supermarket checker, who can take a job which *is* routine from the very start and give it life and meaning.

Questions:

(1) Is there an activity right now for you which has become routine and dull? What is it? Would you like to change it around?

_____

_____

_____

(2) What provides you with a sense of accomplishment? Do you have clear, written, measurable goals for

yourself so that you can track progress or accomplishment?

_____

_____

(3) When was the last time you read, heard, or studied something about your work? What area of your work do you feel you could learn more about?

_____

_____

(4) What activity outside of work gives you a sense of accomplishment? When was the last time you did that activity and how did you reward yourself for its accomplishment?

_____

_____

_____

An insight I have is _____

Actívatíng Agent #2: People Problems

Ah, people. Sometimes we might feel that the world would be much better off without a number of them. The reality is that changing work locations or companies does not always change the people problems. Likewise, if we learn to cope with a difficult person, we have just added that much more power into our bag of magic tricks.

Mary Ellen W. (fictitious name) was hired as the manager in a communications department.

The vice president changed instructions daily, praised Mary Ellen one day for an item, and the next day screamed at her for the very same thing.

Mary Ellen was forbidden to talk with other vice presidents and told that managers were not to be seen in the employee cafeteria. Although asked her opinion, Mary Ellen knew that whatever resulted, the vice president would take all credit and level all blame on the others.

The final straw came when Mary Ellen worked up courage to ask the vice president why the staff would be told one thing and then punished for it. The vice president literally yelled at Mary Ellen and told her to leave the office.

Since Mary Ellen's work was good, the vice president did not fire her, but rather chose the cold/silent treatment and warned the department secretaries that they were to have nothing to do with Mary Ellen other than the most minimal interaction. None of the other senior officers would take on this vice president, and there was no one whom she could go to for a hearing. She left work each day with headaches and earaches.

This *is* a true story. At first blush, it would appear that Mary Ellen should have hightailed it out of there. (The truth is that it is easier to change organizations than it is to change the organization.)

However, Mary Ellen also learned something else. She determined that she would not fall prey to the vice president's plans. Instead, if she could control *her* response to the vice president and play whatever game was required (as long as it was in sync with her ethics and integrity), Mary Ellen would leave if and when *she* was ready.

It worked. And four months later, when Mary Ellen turned in her resignation, the vice president asked her repeatedly to stay.

The point is this: if we can at least control our responses to the problem people in our work life, we stand a much greater chance of making work/job "work" for us.

There are also those people who consider their customers and clients to be "bothers." The difficult ones, the complainers, the know-it-alls, are often just thorns and nothing more. Besides, solving what "bothers" a client is the best way to earn a loyal following.

Questions:

(1) In your current work status, who seems to be able to push those buttons which result in negative responses on your part? A manager, a peer, client, customer?

_____

_____

(2) What situation creates the negative interaction? What do they do?

_____

_____

(3) How do you choose to respond? Are you happy/content with that choice?

_____

_____

(4) I believe that people are basically_____
An insight I have is_____

Activating Agent #3: Work Overload

One of the dilemmas in dealing with work overload is that it has the possibility of being either real or imagined. It is real when someone is literally breathing down our necks, stopwatch in one hand, mounds and pounds of work in the other, saying that "This must be done by...." It is imagined when we *assume* that it must all be done at a specific time, when we have not told the right people just what our situation is, or when our own sense of guilt or fear drives us forward.

Work overload, or the perception of overwork, is serious business because it wears one down to the point of exhaustion. Martin Helldorfer, writing in *The Work Trap,* concludes that overwork can be the product of competency, incompetency, family myth, strong personalities, and/or competitiveness.

Competency

It's not hard to see how the competent person keeps getting more and more of the work. After all, if we're so good at what we do, why don't we just do more? And because we like to buy into and accept that image of The Competent Person, it might be difficult for us to blow the whistle and hold up our hand.

Incompetency

When someone is given work which is beyond his/her capacity, it might also be difficult to admit that help is needed. And so you work very hard at just trying to keep up.

A woman approached me at a seminar with this problem. She was overworked, trying to take medical court cases off a dictating machine. Not only did she not know medical terminology, but she also had never worked the equipment. She had never shared this information with her manager but was, instead, blaming her boss for the amount of work she had to do!

Family Myth

Family myth blends with workload when we grow up thinking that "idle hands are the devil's workshop." Or another myth is, "We pull ourselves up by the bootstraps.

We never ask for help." In the former, we're afraid of legitimate space to rest and breathe. In the latter, we dare not admit that "*more* busy hands make light work."

Strong Personalities

Strong personalities may exert pressure on us because we are afraid to stand up for ourselves ... to let someone know that our endurance level is not the same as theirs.

When I am with a certain colleague, I feel like I am moving in slow motion. Her speed of wit and movement leaves me breathless. She also has the sleeping and eating requirement of a hummingbird. In order to work with her, we have to set some ground rules about what pace I can keep.

Competition

The competitive spirit has not only entered our marketplace, but also the backyard in which we work. Have you ever noticed that some people like to play the "who's busier than who" game. It's rather like seeing who can have the darkest bruise, the most painful headache, the biggest to-do list.

There's an inherent feeling that the busier we are, the more important we must be. Alas, it's a trap that I fall into more times than I care to imagine.

Questions:
(1) What is the work I am *really* suppose to be doing? Have I checked it out with others to see if I am on track?

_____

_____

(2) Do I procrastinate so that there's too much to do in the allotted time? Do I try and get everything finished at once so I can have a clean desk and more work? Am I willing to say, "It is enough"?

_____

_____

_____

(3) Do I compare myself with someone else and try to match his/her pace of work? _____

An insight I have is _____

Activating Agent #4: The Environment

Much has been written about everything from noise to room colors as being potential causes for unpleasant work environments. However, when it comes to individual responsibility, I'm really talking about the actual space we work in—be it an office, a cubicle, even a car. (One woman, unhappy with her work, discovered that as a traveling sales executive, what she really wanted was a desk. She rearranged her car space, put in some creative space-savers in the trunk, and voila! Satisfaction.)

In the case of Bill's kitchen versus Susan's accounting office, one can see that the environment created a feeling of either control or disaster.

Questions:

(1) How would you characterize your current work environment? What can you change? What might you be able to alter further if you think creatively?

_____

_____

(2) Do your work space and materials provide a source of reassurance or dismay? What might make the difference?

_____

_____

An insight I have is_____

Activating Agent #5:
The Morass of Minutiae

Some people get most of their exercise running up molehills—getting all steamed up before they ever find out what's cooking. In short, letting the trivial few become the gargantuan great.

This is a hard activating agent to honestly evaluate because it calls on us to admit that tiny things can drive us crazy.

Questions:
(1) Are there any annoying habits of people whom you work with that bother you? What are those habits? WHY do they bother you?

_____

_____

(2) If you could change anything about your work, what would it be? Which would you do first? The primary items to change—are they major or minutiae?

_____

_____

An insight I have is_____

Activating Agent #6: Hidden Persuaders and Other Baddies

If you thought minutiae was hard, you haven't seen anything yet. This activating agent refers to our beliefs and attitudes about ourselves, work, and people. And since we're here to discover frog factors so that you can begin to acquire the magic of transformation, we're looking at internal attitudes which can hamper us in taking control over where we are now in our lives and letting our work/job "work" for us.

Frankly, I don't know an easy quiz which can instantly produce a clear picture of less-than-optimum attitudes. Nor are there pat answers for overcoming and controlling such hidden persuaders. At best, it seems that if we can begin to uncover and acknowledge powerless attitudes as we become aware of them—or as other people point them out to us—then we stand a chance of changing those attitudes one at a time.

One of the more dangerous hidden persuaders which keeps us feeling helpless and hopeless is a fixed view.

A fixed view is a singular way of seeing something, the proverbial tunnel vision, the one way of interpreting data which says "This is *the* truth." There are always at least two options. *Always.* If I can't change what is, at least I can change how I choose to respond to it. Even no decision is a decision.

Fixed views get us into trouble when we hear ourselves saying things like "there is only one thing to do," or "this is the way I am; take it or leave it."

Fixed views can prompt us into rationalizing non-action. "I can't ask for that. They'll say 'No'." "I better not do such-and-such because this might happen."

The other attitude which also seems pervasive in situations in which we feel like frogs rather than nobility is an habitual pattern of looking for what is negative. We find everything that is wrong with a situation rather than what is right. And our attention focuses on loss rather than gain.

It is said that we teach what we need to learn. I admit to you that I am a learner in overcoming these hidden persuaders.

Questions:

(1) Do you find yourself saying things like "it can't be done", "that's a stupid idea," "what will other people say," "who am I to even consider that?"

_____

(2) Do you find yourself saying things like "but what will happen if," "if only I would have," "I'm just not worthy of any better?"

_____

(3) Do you punish yourself if you try something and it doesn't work, rather than applauding your efforts for making the effort?

_____

An insight I have is_____

The Sorcerer's Apprentice— Basic Magic #101

Having sat in the Magic Castle's room for the "close-at-hand" acts, I've been astounded at the effortless manner in which magicians perform seemingly impossible feats. I'm at a loss to explain it, and I'm sorely tempted to beg one of them to show me "the secret."

Unfortunately, I also know that even if they were to give me a look at the mechanism involved in their magic, I would still not be able to replicate the trick. Only years of practice, patience, and perseverance have resulted in their skill.

That's a healthy analogy to take with us on this journey of making wherever we are in life "work" for us so that we can begin to move closer into living our dreams and using our gifts. There is no one-step abracadabra. By the same token, I also believe that the magic needed to transform our lives and our work is tucked away in all of us. It's not reserved for the peak performers but is available to all of us if we only take the time and effort to consider options and actions which, though small, can be powerful.

That's a key word, "actions." Let's get going.

Summary

1. There is no ideal job. The magic is not in the work but in the worker.
2. What makes the difference between frogs and princes(ess) is not the task but where they choose to concentrate their energy.
3. In order to begin to get control over where we *are* in our work life so that we can move to what *can be,* it is necessary to identify frog factors— activating agents which create a sense of power- lessness.
4. The more common activating agents are:
   - Going through the motions—routine, boredom, no challenge
   - People problems

- Work overload
- The environment
- Hidden persuaders and other baddies.

THOUGHT TO CONTEMPLATE: My life is a river. If I could see it from the highest peak, I would recognize the white water, the oxbow lakes, the thick slow currents, the gentle expanse that feeds into one ocean. I will bloom where I am planted; and tomorrow, when I have taken all that I can from this place and given all I can, I will send forth a new seed. It will move down the river to the next place where it will catch hold and I will grow again ... more powerful than before because I made the most of where I came from.

Chapter Three

How To Recognize A Pit When You're In One

Sometimes I wish I just had a summer job here.

—John F. Kennedy
(to students working in Washington)

You should see me now. Seated before a computer keyboard in a friend's office, I am attempting to use her compatible software program. The computer part is easy. It's her scruffy, pumpkin-colored cat curled in my lap that makes reaching the keyboard so difficult. Crazy cat. I've tried countless times to remove him (or is it her?) but crazy cat (C.C.) keeps coming back.

C.C. just can't be *that* comfortable. Every time I strike a key, its head bounces back and forth in the crook of my arm. The furry bottom slops over my thighs and its neck tilts perpendicularly to its spine. Yet Crazy Cat stays.

It strikes me that a number of us are much like my

feline lap-warmer. We'll frequently stay in a job of dubious "comfort" either by preferring the pain of the position to the perceived agony of change or by convincing ourselves that this is the best we can expect.

Or there are those of us who resemble the restless tomcat I see prowling around my friend's garden. Antsy and nervous, this fellow can't seem to find whatever he's looking for anywhere. I have a feeling that if he could talk, he'd loudly complain about everyone and everything. No matter where he goes, nothing is ever right.

Tomcat is like those wandering folks who can't quite focus on what is wrong with a job and therefore, everything is wrong. And it is always someone else's fault and not theirs that (sigh!) jobs are always so unfair and life is a sketchy place with only crumbs of happiness.

To complete the analogy, I note a mechanical cat sitting on the book shelf. If I wind the toy up tight, it will run in circles, be the epitome of a perfect cat, and stop dead in its tracks when the metal spring is exhausted. (Sound like anyone you might know?)

Please understand that I'm not being cynical or snide. Somehow it's easier for us to think of the symptoms of others before we can apply them to ourselves.

Hence the necessity of this chapter. A doctor would never look for the cause and possible treatment of illness without first getting a list of symptoms. Neither can we.

There's also an ulterior motive in this chapter. If you bought this book, you're already aware that something is not clicking within your work/life or else you're looking to make what is good even better. But if someone bought this book for you, there's a very good chance that your friend is seeing an unhappy situation in which you are knowingly or unknowingly involved. Perhaps the following stories of real people might trigger a simultaneous "Why, that's me!" reaction.

The Difference Between
A Pit and a Pothole

Learning to recognize the real symptoms of a pit—and not the more shallow lows of a pothole—is critical. Let me explain.

A pothole symbolizes those down times that are to be expected of ANY job or work: pressure deadlines on a project, a new routine, a change in management, the presence of tasks which just aren't our favorites, a difficult individual, etc. The nice thing about potholes is that it's relatively easy to get out of them. I can see over the rim into daylight. In fact, maybe I know the road so well, I even know when they're coming and can prepare for it. And I CAN climb out.

For example, I truly enjoy speaking before audiences, giving workshops and seminars, and facilitating group dynamics. However, to do those things, I must spend time marketing my services—a task which I consider a pothole—a necessary evil.

Prior to writing this book, I experienced another pothole. A client gave me six weeks to develop and write a proposal in answer to a government solicitation. Every day, seven days a week, twelve to seventeen hours a day, I labored. The end result was 752 pages plus the mental state of a zombie. A true pothole. But if I did this type of work as a standard practice (and there are companies which do nothing but write proposals with horrendous deadlines), then I know—for me—I'd be in a pit.

Potholes are generally those things which can be either tolerated, rearranged, or even removed. However, the people like Mr. Tomcat spend most of the time creating an imagined pit from potholes.

Case in point: At the conclusion of a workshop I had given on coping with difficult people, a secretary came up to me and gravely complained about how bad her boss and work were. Her complaint: the boss made changes after she gave him the final copy of letters! "And I have to redo letters so often. It drives me crazy."

Yes, the secretary had a word processor. She rarely had to stay past regular hours. Yes, she received overtime. She just didn't like typing something over.

See what I mean? In her mind, she had turned a pothole into a pit. Other than provide some advice for restructuring the letter-writing process and communicating with the boss in a problem-solving manner, I could only inwardly wonder why she was a secretary in the first place. That seemed to be the true issue.

But a pit—now that's real trouble. There's no blue sky, no way out. It's nothing that can be tolerated, rearranged, or removed. The symptoms range from helpless frustration and apathy to rage or tremendous effort with little results (much like Mechanical Cat). But across the board, there is a feeling (even if denied) of not being in control; of *continually* not being in balance. I stress continually because potholes can also throw us out of whack, but only temporarily.

The Pit Process

When I was six, I got the mumps. Mother knew it as soon as I couldn't swallow a pickle. I probably ran a fever, definitely developed chipmunk cheeks, and enjoyed lying in bed and coloring. However, if I had gotten the mumps at age thirty-five, the symptoms would have been more severe and the recovery less pleasant.

The symptoms of a pit will also vary as we grow through our jobs or work. Depending upon where we are at this particular time in our lives, the pit will manifest itself in different forms. And there will be numerous pits with each stage of growth.

A Word About The Case Studies

Experience is a great teacher. This book contains firsthand or composite accounts about the experiences of others, what worked, and what failed. In this chapter, the case studies detail symptoms, just symptoms. See how each person behaved, how he or she felt, and what other areas of life were impacted during this "pit" stage. Record any similarities you might feel. Remember, without isolating the symptoms, you won't be able to determine if a solution works.

The Granddaddy Of Pits—Burnout

Ever since New York psychologist Dr. Herbert J. Freudenberger popularized the phrase "burn-out" in 1980, the term has become a catchall for a host of discontents ranging from the workplace to the homefront. And probably for good reason. Look at his definition:

"Burn-out: To deplete oneself. To exhaust one's physical and mental resources. To wear oneself out by excessively striving to reach some unrealistic expectation imposed by one's self or by the values of society."

_._

He further expands this definition by calling burnout, *"a state of fatigue or frustration brought about by devotion to a cause, a way of life, or relationship that failed to produce the expected rewards."*

What we see in this definition is the high achiever, the perfectionist, the workaholic, the goal-oriented idealist who demands the optimum out of every experience and maybe everybody. In my mind, I also visualize the "burned-out" individual as someone who has become out of balance by devotion or monumental striving in doing the real or perceived "work" of their lives.

Freudenberger serves as a perfect example. During the sixties, he set up a free clinic in the East Village of New York City to help the dropping-out, young flower children. Beset by drugs, illness, lack of money and fear, the youth streamed into his clinic.

After completing a full day at his regular practice, this kindly psychologist would rush to the free clinic and stay until the early morning hours. He became obsessed with making the clinic work. At home (when he was home), his family members were met with irritability and a short temper. His friends anxiously inquired about his health. He angrily denied their observations. The turning point came when, instead of packing to go on a Christmas vacation with his wife and children, Freudenberger fell sound asleep for two solid days!

Small wonder that from his personal experience with burnout caused by over-dedication to his true work and unrealistic self-expectations, Dr. Freudenberger became a leader in understanding this prevalent modern-day problem. Small wonder, too, that I highly recommend his book, *Burn-Out: How to Beat the High Cost of Success.*

❧

Janet E., assistant magazine publisher.

Hired fresh out of college to serve as editor on an up-and-coming slick city magazine, Janet bent to the task with vigor. She accepted everything that came down the line: all editing, the art department, the cover story, even typesetting. She put in seventy hours a week, juggled a marriage, and within two years "the work was the same, but I wasn't. I felt used, had no confidence and little self-esteem. There was no acknowledgment of what I was doing. No reward. The publisher was into sales but not content. She'd jump up and down over a big ad sale but never read my articles. I had no feedback. I felt I was an editor taking little steps instead of a really good editor taking giant leaps."

Working harder wasn't doing the trick. Nor were the obsessive games of solitaire which she played at home rather than talk with her husband. She felt trapped financially.

"I was using my salary to surround myself with luxuries—to forget work. I was spending money to make money, as a substitute for what was missing in my daily routine."

Then one day, she heard a giant, bottom-of-the-soul sigh. "I looked around. There was no one there. It had come from me." Without telling her husband, she quit her job.

Dr. A. O'Donnell (fictitious name), radiologist, late forties.

Absolutely fascinating. There are no other words to describe Dr. O'Donnell. From photography, to literature, to music, to world events, Dr. O'Donnell can command any group with his experiences and knowledge. He is well-respected in his field, keeps up with every journal publication, and is part of a highly respected hospital that grows by leaps and bounds, However, no new radiologists are added to the business. The consortium does not want to dilute the income and Dr. O'Donnell has bills, many bills.

One work shift rolls into another. Perfection is demanded. Play is a forgotten word. So is the time spent with his wife. She questions his exhaustion, the tension, the strain. His response: "One cannot admit being on the edge." It is a conspiracy of silence among the doctors.

Seeking professional guidance in dealing with the stress is seen as a sign of weakness and instability. Energy must be spent to keep up the pretense of superhuman ability.

At last, friends and loved ones are pushed away. The relentless grind continues. Dr. O'Donnell literally disappears from the sight of anyone not immediately connected with the hospital.

More About Burnout

In looking at these stories, we can isolate more subtle symptoms: fatigue, despondence, a rejection of others, an unwillingness to talk about feelings, a push to do more than what can reasonably be expected, the rejection of time for relaxation, a sense of helplessness, and certainly denial.

Try this little quiz suggested by Dr. Freudenberger and see how you fare. Don't spend more than 30 seconds on each question. Your initial reaction is normally the most accurate.

Think about the last six months and then rank each response on a scale of 1 (rarely true) to 5 (definitely true).

1. Do you tire more easily? Feel fatigued rather than energetic? _____.
2. Are people annoying you by telling you, "You don't look so good lately"? _____.
3. Are you working harder and harder and accomplishing less? _____.
4. Are you increasingly cynical and disenchanted? _____.
5. Are you often invaded by a sadness you can't explain? _____.
6. Are you forgetting appointments, deadlines, personal possessions? _____.
7. Are you increasingly irritable? More short-tempered? More disappointed in the people around you? _____.
8. Are you seeing close friends and family members less frequently? _____.
9. Are you too busy to do routine things like make phone calls, read reports or send out Christmas cards? _____.
10. Are you suffering from physical complaints? _____.
11. Do you feel disoriented when the activity of the day comes to a halt? _____.
12. Is joy elusive? _____.
13. Are you unable to laugh at a joke about yourself? _____.
14. Does sex seem like more trouble than it's worth? _____.
15. Do you have very little to say to people? _____.

The Burnout Scale

0-25	You're doing fine.
26-35	There are things you should be watching.
36-50	You're a candidate.
51-65	You are burning out.
Over 65	You're in a dangerous place, threatening to your physical and mental well-being.

"Keep in mind that this is merely an approximation of where you are, useful as a guide on your way to a more satisfying life. Don't let a high total alarm you, but pay attention to it. Burnout is reversible, no matter how far along it is. The higher number signifies that the sooner you start being kind to yourself, the better." [Freudenberger, Dr. Herbert J. and Richelson, Geraldine, *Burn-Out: How to Beat the High Cost of Success* (New York: Doubleday and Company, 1980.)]

Beyond Burnout

An observation: One does not have to be a high-achiever, a relentless striver, or a potential burnout victim to be in the pits; to feel that life is out of control and tasteless. In short, one does not have to burn out before taking stock of the situation and figuring out corrective action.

It also seems to me that there are subtle distinctions as well as similarities between true burnouts and other "pits."

You'll see what I mean in the following case histories.

The Empty-Feeling Pit

When we were kids and played hide-and-seek inside on rainy days, it was generally some object instead of one of us that hid. I can still hear the clues as we wandered around the living room: "Naw, you're cold. Better now. Getting warmer. Nope, cooled off. Now you're hot. getting hotter...."

Mother had another way of saying it. We were "in the right church but the wrong pew." So it is with the pit that comes from being "warm" in discovering your "work" or in handling your "job." You're in the right general area, but not quite there yet. There's discontent, anxiety, maybe even disappointment. Something just isn't right. At the place next to your heart, it seems very empty.

Robert W., psychotherapist.

One brief conversation with Robert and you become very glad that his mother didn't triumph with dentistry. His bristly black beard contrasts against gentle blue eyes that crinkle with warmth when he listens and guides individuals through personal life transitions. His talent is counseling; a gift that surely would have been lost on dental crowns and upper bridge plates.

But it has taken Robert years of his own movement through pits to arrive at a place where his "work" fits and that empty feeling has been replaced by internal satisfaction and creative expression.

By 1970, with a masters in psychiatric social work, Robert was well established in Beverly Hills as a psychotherapist and family counselor. The "pew" certainly looked right: XKE Jaguar, apartment with a prestigious address, married to a gorgeous therapist, enough clients to have a second home in Laguna Beach. But something was missing. "We had been to enough charming dinner parties in homes with Spanish live-in maids to have tired of that. I looked at others in the profession who had larger houses, were chairmen of departments, had bigger practices, and I asked myself, if I get to be them, will I be happy? I got to see that none of those things would give me what I was looking for."

His significance in life seemed too shallow, without meaning. In spite of external signs of success, a feeling of incompleteness led him to continual searching. In the big picture, where and why did he belong?

⚜

Cheryl P., former director of communications of a professional association.

Unlike many of us who just fell into our first occupations without any clear-cut purpose, Cheryl's earliest memories were of writing. "My mother still has the news clipping of some essay contest I won in first grade," she chuckled. "They probably printed every entry."

For the later-to-become reporter, it was her first of many newspaper clippings. But it would take the reoccurrence of pits and repeated attempts before she figured out just what form her writing career was to take.

It took seven years on the news and feature beats of two daily newspapers for the first round of symptoms. "The stories weren't interesting any more. Even the features didn't stimulate me. I was just plain bored. That's when I thought about going into public relations—something related to writing but a new world. But even though I interviewed with a firm, I still wasn't ready to give up my identity as a reporter. There's something very romantic about being a reporter. People look at you with such interest. It's a hard role to give up."

But a year later, the boredom had doubled and cynicism crept in. "Sluggish, unenthused—yes, that's how I felt. The challenge was gone for some reason. I'd find my mind drifting in interviews, wanting to sleep in city council meetings. I wasn't interested in what I was writing and neither, I discovered, were a lot of people.

And I wanted something positive. As a reporter you generally do look for the worst, for the bad news, and go in with that attitude. That was another aspect—reporters being objective. The longer I worked, the more I realized that they aren't and that's hard to live with. I could feel myself becoming cynical about both my personal and professional life."

A brief stint with a public relations firm and Cheryl headed for executive ranks with the title of director of communications for a major medical association. Within three years, new symptoms were present.

"By the end of the first year, I started missing the writing. I got so involved in meetings that there was never time to write well. Between meetings and politics, I found I wasn't very comfortable. Something kept nagging at me, telling me 'You're unhappy because you're not writing. That's what you enjoy most.'

"I hated to go into work. I hated the pressure of knowing that I now had a mortgage payment over my head. There was a bad bout with the flu and my throat had a feeling of tightness which the doctor said was related to the autonomic nervous system ... I could swallow fine but there was this sensation. In one sense, I was relieved when the doctor said it was stress. But in the other sense I felt helpless. And my stomach aches seemed to grow each day I was there. I just felt that I really wasn't doing what maybe I was best at. I could do whatever they gave me to do, but I wasn't enjoying it. And I didn't like managing people at all."

The End-Of-The-Road Pit

There's another form of pit which comes when you are faced with the fact that you're probably not even in the right "church," let alone pew. You've done it all, accomplished whatever the task was (maybe with much success), and a long path of nothingness faces you in the night. There is no opportunity for moving up or down ... only out. The empty feeling next to your heart is also accompanied by an ache at the base of your spine.

The base of your spine is considered to be the location for the energy to bring things into reality, to create, to give life. When the ache is centered there, confusion, dismay and maybe even despair can seem overwhelming. There's a sense of having nothing to show for the effort expended.

George G. (fictitious name), recently retired senior executive for a multinational corporation, learned that birthrights can be dangerous things. At least so it seems to George, an impressive silver-haired gentleman whose good looks knock years off his age and belie the fact that he grew up during the Great Depression.

Coming from an era where job security meant sticking with one company until you accepted a plaque and a Timex watch (Rolex, if the company was a star performer on the New York Stock Exchange), George's story is brief but poignant. From a journalism degree, he entered his uncle's company and rose to become vice president of public relations, advertising, and industrial relations. But at the beginning of his second decade with the firm, he quit. The dilemma: personal worthiness.

"By materialistic standards, I had it made. But I felt unappreciated. My career had peaked. And I doubted my ability. Did I get where I was because of the good fairy who made me or was I competent? I was anxious, depressed. My marriage was falling apart, even though its demise didn't happen for another ten years. But most of all, I felt it would really die if I didn't do something."

Gary R., former executive in the recording industry.

At the time Gary encountered his most significant pit, this middle-aged father of two teenage daughters had come quite a long way for a high school dropout from Brooklyn. His accounting degree earned in night school and his quick understanding of the music industry pushed Gary up the ladder of the recording business. Almost each career decision had been made with wisdom and good timing. But now, earning six figures as an executive for a national trade publication for the recording industry, the end-of-the-road pit appeared.

With the company moving its headquarters from California to New York, the job as director of business affairs was changing. Budgetary functions, licensing agreements, departmental liaisons were gone. Life became routine. "Every day became less challenging, less enjoyable, less exciting. I was more involved in handling the company's conventions, but it wasn't enough to fill the void. I felt trapped, frustrated, angry, upset, annoyed. The promised new publication and attendant challenges did not appear. What was the way out??" Gary wasn't even sure he wanted to remain in the industry which had pleased him for so long.

⚜

Charles D., former president of a marketing corporation.

Well over twenty years ago, Charles entered the infant home improvement industry with his ideas for marketing and sales just tumbling around in creative juices. It only took eight years in the corporate world to convince this young executive that the grass was greener in his own back yard. "So I started a marketing company for the industry, representing manufacturers and retailers, training store people, warehousing goods, and developing merchandising techniques."

Within ten years, the company had grown from nothing to around $6 million in yearly revenue. But

Charles was antsy, ill-at-ease. "I lost interest in the business. Started dabbling in psychology classes at night. I really didn't have anything planned beyond my company. And so I plodded along, half-hearted. The company kept growing. The decision of what to do with my work got more difficult. We had a nice big building, an impressive office. I was like a king holding court. But it wasn't doing it for me. I thought of ways to phase down, to go part time, to ask my partner to run the company, but nothing worked.

There was no joy. Selling tool boxes to home-fixer-uppers just didn't do it for me. I was afraid to leave. So I spent three years trying to juggle reality, putting on a patch that wasn't working, trying to reconcile myself that it was really time to move on." The role of a hot-shot, high-powered company president was moving stage left.

The I-Wanna-Be-Me Pit

Once you understand what is your "work" (i.e., that which excites and has meaning for you), the closer you come to being in a pit if you cannot perform that "work" as either an after-job activity or as part of the job. Assume you truly delight in working with people and in solving personnel problems and yet your job has you seated all day at a computer terminal. Because of a long commute, you're too tired at night to do anything but eat and sleep. Chances are you'll be feeling any or all of the symptoms mentioned in the other pits.

Note the difference between this and the Empty Pit. In the Empty Pit, you *are* doing what appears to be the mean-ingful work of your life and yet you want more. In the I-

Wanna-Be-Me Pit, you are not getting to do that "work" at all.

The Potpourri Pit

While the other "pits" have more individual character and symptoms and seem to require dramatic action, we also experience a state of non-living when we're out of balance for a multitude of reasons. It's the old trying-to-keep-seven-balls-in-the-air-at-once routine, probably compounded if you want a standing ovation for a perfect performance at the end.

※

Ronda S., former language/speech and hearing specialist.

With a gift for gab, a credential in communication disorders, and some bilingual skills in Spanish, Ronda delighted in her school position. But the pressure of a special-education environment with overwhelming paperwork left Ronda feeling constantly behind.

"I tried to re-structure the situation by transferring to a year-round school to see if a regular break would relieve the stress. For the first few years that switch helped. With four vacations a year, I had a sense that I had four beginnings."

The school itself was exciting: There were high-powered professionals on staff, an innovative principal, a model program as a community school, childcare for mothers, a foster grandparent program, and a strong volunteer group. Still looking for more challenges, Ronda also volunteered for additional work at the district level. Although admittedly spread too thin, it took a divorce to really put the imbalance wheels in motion.

"I'm not extravagant, but without a second income I needed additional funds to stay in my California home. So for about a year, I worked after hours teaching six Japanese families. I'd find myself drained at the end of a day. I realized that from morning to night I was encouraging people to communicate. I had about twelve therapy groups, didn't take a full lunch, and then left the school to teach again. I was attempting to inspire people all day long. When I did get home, to keep up social contact with my friends, I'd spend hours on the phone. I was overwhelmed with communication."

She again attempted to alter her environment, cutting out phone calls, taking lunches, but the imbalance continued. Another pressure was added: romance. "After being single for nearly four years, I was involved in a crazy romance with someone living on the East Coast. We felt strongly about the relationship, so, once again, there were require-ments—writing, planning trips, travel. He finally moved within some seventy-five miles of me, but then there were weekend commutes. I also sold my house and within six months I had moved three times.

By Christmas of that year, I realized I wasn't in control—working two jobs, commuting every weekend, not being committed to an exercise program. I had stomach pains, but the tests for an ulcer were negative. It wasn't just the work that was in the pits. It was everything!"

The People Pit

Have you ever been invited as a first-time guest to a meeting, a party, or a dinner where you discovered that you weren't quite comfortable with the other people? Or do you remember, at least once in your education, a teacher whom you barely tolerated through a semester? The mix was like oil and water.

Just because we're now grown up (make that "growing up"), it doesn't mean that we won't encounter such groups or individuals in our work/job lives. In most cases, I believe such people are truly only "potholes" who can be handled, *but,* I also believe there are those few instances where the presence of an individual or a specific corporate culture can evoke all the symptoms of a pit: fatigue, anger, inability to work effectively, illness, despondency, even despair. It is brought on not by the everyday tasks at hand, but by human interaction.

⚜

Mary B. (fictitious name) industrial relations director, "Big Board" corporation.

Mary generally loved her work. When she could travel and do hands-on assistance at plants away from corporate headquarters, she shined. But daily work at the home office had become a trial by fire.

She answered directly to the vice president of communications, a man who insisted upon a rigid adherence to his personal management style, who took sole credit for any good idea generated from the department, and who would laugh one minute and then fly into rages and yell the next. Employees tiptoed around. Mary never knew which end was up.

In her then-fifteen-year career, she had never encountered such behavior, nor such restraints.

Then one day Mary made the mistake of correcting the vice president. He flew into a rage and accused Mary of trying to sabotage the department. Mary left, gulping down the anger.

In the weeks to follow, the vice president coldly ignored her. The department secretary came in to tell Mary that the vice president had warned other employees to stay away from her. Mary was distraught. She'd go home in knots. There were constant headaches.

Mary had moved across the country to take the job and had no other area contacts. Corporate policy, as dictated by the vice president, prohibited her from joining professional organizations which met during the day. She felt trapped and alone.

The Dimensions of Pits

Just as a fever can range anywhere above 98.6 degrees, so too can the symptoms of being in a pit vary in intensity. Some days are harder than others; some pits deeper than others. Some symptoms can be overcome in hours while others might take years. But the most important thing in beginning a journey of self-discovery and self-growth is the recognition that where you are now in your work life is not where you want to be.

I must hasten to add a postscript here. Some "pits" occur literally and figuratively overnight: job termination, bankruptcy, divorce, death of a spouse or a significant person. Because of the special trauma created by such tragedies, Chapter Five is reserved just for handling these cases. But regardless of why a pit is present, the same opportunity for personal growth and the same process of exploration apply.

Throughout the rest of the book, you'll discover what most of the aforementioned people as well as others did to understand and alter the current course of their lives.

Summary

1. Too often we fail to acknowledge the symptoms of a pit or even a pothole because we are afraid to change.

2. Some people make pits out of potholes. A pothole is the to-be-expected negative side of any work or job. (I might love selling, but I hate filling out sales reports.)

3. A pothole can be tolerated, arranged, or even removed.

4. A pit is a mental and physical state of being which cannot be tolerated, which cannot be ignored, which has resulted in imbalance throughout all corners of your life.

5. Burnout, the pit of high achievers, perfectionists, and workaholics, is the exhaustion of one's energies brought about by striving to reach some unrealistic goal or by devotion to a way of life that fails to produce the the expected reward.

6. One can be in a pit without having burned out.

7. The primary symptom of the Empty-Feeling Pit is exactly that—a feeling of being "not filled" with enough of the chosen work.

8. The primary symptom of the End-of-the-Road Pit is a feeling of being lost and confused in

determining what might be your "work."

9. The primary symptom of the I-Wanna-Be-Me Pit is frustration because there is no allowance for your "work" in any part of your life.

10. The Potpourri Pit is a collection of symptoms stemming from imbalance in multiple areas besides your work/job.

11. You might be in a pit with your current employment if you experience some of the following symptoms: constant fatigue, reluctance to go to work, lack of motivation, boredom, sadness, irritability (either at home or at your place of employment), increased use of alcohol, drugs, or cigarettes, despondency, despair, constant complaining, inability to laugh, illicit sex, crying jags, medical complaints (head, stomach, neck, back, throat), continual denial when asked if anything is wrong, forgetfulness, little time for play, for friends or self, and an unwillingness to share feelings.

Chapter Four

Okay, It's a Pit—
Now What?

— · — · — · — · — · — · — · — · — · — · — · —

If you do not change your direction, you are
likely to end up where you are headed.
—*Ancient Chinese Proverb*

From the ruins of ancient civilization, archaeologists
have uncovered human skulls with a small hole bored into
the forehead. It is theorized that early surgeons sought to
relieve migraine headaches by allowing the evil matter
and/or demons to escape through the opening. Pretty drastic
measure for someone suffering from a pounding cranium.
But then I guess any action was preferred to pain. And there
certainly was a change for the patient: a number even lived
with new bone growing over the gaping hole!

I relate this tale to put the wisdom of the Orient into
perspective. The proverb quoted in the beginning of this
chapter rightfully implies that unless action is taken—

unless a change is made—things will stay exactly as they are.

May I suggest that MANY changes are possible without resorting to radical surgery. You have more options than our hole-in-the-head ancestors. Those early neurosurgeons performed the operations because they were aware of only one cause of the pain. In reality, there were many.

So too will there probably be a number of causes for the symptoms, the imbalance, the non-living feeling which we might encounter in our work/job lives. The purpose of this chapter is to provide guidance in helping you to determine just what might be some causes for the pit or imbalance as well as steps which various individuals have found helpful in exploring potential changes in direction.

First Stage: Analysis Of Situation

Accept responsibility for your role in the pit.

In the first chapter, I listed four attitudes which could prevent someone from even beginning to look at work and life. To think that one is perpetually programmed by an educational track, that success can only be defined by money (and the converse attitude that only the shallow can avidly seek riches), and that mistakes are taboo, are all limiting attitudes.

There are other attitudes derived from our perceptions of life which also create tiny, airless boxes into which we stuff our souls. The good news is that we have the power to burst out of these boxes.

However, what happens so easily is that we give away our power. Often, without even knowing it, we let others have control over what we do and how we feel. And then someone or something outside of us takes the blame.

At down times, the internal conversations with ourselves might go something like this:

"Okay, job—I'm miserable and it's your fault. You did it, not me."

"Boss, make me happy. You're responsible for knowing what I need."

"It's my wife's fault that I must work so hard. She wants expensive things."

"Everybody wants everything yesterday. If I'm going to keep this job, I have to please everyone."

"I'm too old to change. I hate what I'm doing but I can't give up my lifestyle."

Pretty powerless monologue. But it doesn't have to be. You helped create your situation and therefore you also have the power to re-create it. You are not a victim of circumstance. You are not helpless. But first you must determine just how you are contributing to the "pit."

Response To Personal History

Each of us has his own mental scrapbook of experiences which can influence our choices in positive and negative ways. Remember the scene from "Gone With the Wind" when a starving Scarlett O'Hara frantically digs through the burned earth, finds a carrot and swears, "With God as my witness, I'll never be hungry again."?

From that point on, Scarlett's actions are predicated on the fact that she chooses to feel she never has enough. She always wants more clothes, money, food, admirers and therefore creates the situations to respond to that experience.

In real life, one might also give more power than is deserved to personal experiences.

When Dr. Freudenberger began examining the causes for his burnout, he realized that the very idea of a clinic for flower children came as a result of his exceedingly difficult childhood in Nazi Germany. He over-identified with the youth of the sixties who elected to slip away from the norms of society. There was, in fact, little correlation between those young adults and the German youth who were pursued by the Gestapo and made homeless by a national holocaust.

Another example:

Susan, age forty (composite), an attorney.

Ever since passing the bar she has successfully scratched and clawed her way through cases which few lawyers would have won. Although there has been little time for significant relationships, she always finds time to write home about each case, enclosing her news clippings as often as possible.

Her dad is thinking of retiring and expects Susan to come home to take over his legal practice. She can't put her finger on it, but lately she's been getting severe headaches and finding that she is almost too wound up to sleep. Friends seldom call her because she abruptly tells them "I have to go now. I'm too busy."

With the help of a counselor, Susan is beginning to realize how much she has allowed a personal experience to color her life, to create her pit by living out the life of a dead brother.

When she was ten years old, her only brother died of leukemia. Her parents were devastated, particularly her father. He had often talked about the family law practice, which had been started back in the 1800s, and how Tommy would help carry on the tradition. After the funeral, her dad started to cry. She was crushed to see tears streaming down his face. From that moment on, Susan determined that her dad would never be hurt again.

Although she has enjoyed the practice of law, Susan now feels trapped by the thought of maintaining her practice in the family's small hometown. Furthermore, she has begun to feel alone and empty in her work—thus trying to work harder to make up for the loss.

Although not all personal history is as dramatic as the incidents above, I think the message is clear. We can't change direction until we decide just how much control we have allowed people or events to have over our lives.

Yes, I agree with poet John Donne when he says, "I am a part of all that I have met." But this does not mean that who we are and what we do must be determined by forces *outside* of us. Flavored, yes. Cast in stone, no. That would make living reactive instead of pro-active.

Response To Social Pressure

The common thread which runs through all pits is a feeling (even if denied) of being out of control or out of balance. Another cause for that feeling could be the fact that one is attempting to satisfy the collective wish of a group.

Probably today's most prevalent social pressure comes from the movement of women into both higher and newer positions. Instead of the social pressure to be a contented housewife and mother, the push is for independence, status, and title.

Downstown by Tim Downs

Cheryl determined that her acceptance of such pressure was contributing to the pit. "I tried to convince myself that I should be an executive. That I had it made. Me, a director of communications. But that was someone else's expectation—not mine.

"I became aware that one of my inner struggles was trying to live up to the 'whole' woman—climb the ladder. But it wasn't me."

Another woman plugged away for over a decade as an urban planner before she wised up to the fact that her dissatisfaction came because all along she had wanted to be a teacher. But teaching had been stereotyped as a female profession, so she opted for a non-traditional role.

As the *Downstown* cartoon so tersely relates, what counts most for living is not the status of upward mobility of our work/job, but rather our happiness. For both men and women, the pressure to be a "success" often overshadows "being happy."

Response To Ethical Considerations

The question here is not what business you are in, but rather what business practices are involved. Interestingly enough, I have encountered cases where subjects were unaware that part of the intrinsic cause of their uncomfortable position was a personal conflict with the work they were called upon to do.

> *Maureen C. (composite), accounts payable clerk for a prominent hotel.*

Every night, Maureen comes home just exhausted. It seems she is always behind in her work and that the most hated portion of her job is telling vendors that they must wait to be paid.

"The worse part is that I know what the owners take out of the business. They have a fancy house and just bought a limousine. Yet I have to keep inventing excuses because we're often months in arrears."

In her personal life, Maureen pays each bill as soon as it arrives in the mail. Yet her inability to control vendor payment creates a dilemma.

⁂

> *John W. (composite) sells circuit boards for an engineering company.*

John prides himself on answering all phone calls, following up on inquiries, and placing accurate orders. But once the orders hit the assembly process, he loses control of the client's order. Sometimes shipments are delayed or lost. John has promised the goods and feels personally responsible for the delinquent account. The company can't always deliver in the fashion he thinks is needed.

If a portion of John's personal sense of integrity is linked to the delivery of a product, then John must become very clear on how much control he needs, and if such control is ever even possible in a sales

position. Without that understanding, one cause of
John's pit will be unresolved.

Response to Self-Image
and Self-Esteem

Self-image is the picture you hold of yourself. Based
upon that picture (which may be distorted), you take action.
Remember Janet E., the assistant publisher? She felt incompetent and ill-equipped for her job. Her resultant action
which contributed to the burnout was to assume more tasks
than were humanly possible and to work a tremendous
number of hours.

The hidden agenda behind some out-of-control
workers is to imagine that longer hours, more duties, or
heavier workloads will increase the depleted confidence or
negative self-image. Until one comes to grips with the
internal cause behind burnout, the scenario will be repeated
from job, to job, to job.

Another dangerous self-image is that of the Hopeless
Hannah or Helpless Howard. These are well-meaning folk
who got the message early on that only "luck" or "getting a
break" controls the world. And so they never ask for what
they want. According to former career consultant Barbara
Abrams Mintzer, the people who don't go out of the pit to
seek the job/work they want are not only afraid of rejection,
but they've already rejected themselves!

Self-esteem is the value you give yourself. The
perfectionist, the relentless striver, the Wonder Woman and
Superman frequently feel that unless work/job is done
according to exterior signs of success, they have no
personal worth. This might be compounded by a sense that

no one can do it but them. Additionally, while they might exude confidence, their problem is multiplied by a self-image which demands only pinnacles and no plateaus. Omnipotence is a killer task master.

At face value, this might seem contradictory. True, we've established that our job or work is the primary source of personal identity and that "work" is that activity which puts meaning and energy into our lives. But, that does not imply our *value,* our *worthiness* as human beings, is determined by the success of our efforts.

Our work or job should never be the single determinant of self-esteem. Unless we separate our being from work, we will always be vulnerable to any professional setback, criticism, or negative feedback.

Determine Level of Expectations of Work/Job

Consider this reality testing. Ask yourself if what is being expected of you (or what you expect of yourself) is reasonable. Remember, frequently the "pit" comes from over-dedication, over-exhaustion for a perfectly legitimate reason.

In Dr. Freudenberger's case, not only was it unreasonable to expect himself to work night and day, but the clinic was understaffed, the number of clients too great, the community support lacking.

Our other burnout victim, Dr. A. O'Donnell, is being called upon to attend patients without having sufficient opportunity to rest and regroup. Additionally, since his personal expectation is that he must also keep current with journals, whatever little time he has is spent in educational reading. Both the personal and professional expectations are severely tilted. When this is coupled with an abandonment of personal power to do anything but remain within the vicious cycle, the outlook is grim. Sad to report, until Dr. O'Donnell or someone else within that medical community cries "enough," the pit remains.

A word of caution. It's mighty easy to turn a pothole into a pit when it comes to expectations. Could it be that you are grinding yourself into a pit when, in fact, that is not what is expected of you at all? Have you created more burden for yourself than necessary? Or are you turning reasonable expectations into burdens because you don't quite belong in that role?

Determine if the "Pit" Is Really Work/Job

Because we spend most of our waking moments in a place of employment, it is understandable that we are inclined to consider work as our central reason for non-living.

Work can be the scapegoat. In fact, it might be a good cover-up for what is the real root of unhappiness and a feeling of imbalance. I know. I did it. In my first real go-around with a pit, I considered the fact that I was bored, uncomfortable, unchallenged, and without joy as being solely the result of work. "That's it," I thought. "I need different work. I need challenge, something new."

Thankfully, somewhere between cleaning up my résumé and beginning a cursory exploration program, I realized what was really wrong. I had no business doing anything else until I came to grips with my marriage. Only the resolution of the real cause for my pit allowed an authentic opportunity to seek work and balance.

Work or a job might also be the cover-up for a denial of health issues. The man who decides that chest pains, headaches, and mood swings are the result of work might really be carrying a time bomb inside that will go off regardless of where and how he works. While job stress and physical ailments can be symptoms of being in a pit, conversely such ailments can still be signs that something is indeed wrong physically. A chemical imbalance might be the root cause for an individual going through several jobs, always finding the tasks too stressful and fatigue being a constant companion. Correct this imbalance and work becomes easier. The pit has been filled in.

One of the harder health issues to handle is alcoholism. Although massive efforts are under way to educate the public about this disease, the usual response of a sufferer is denial. The job becomes the cause of tension, depression, conflicts with fellow employees and managers, difficulty in handling the job responsibilities. In reality, the disease of alcoholism is the true culprit.

Once again, even in this step, introspection and the willingness to honestly look at our contribution to the "pit" becomes paramount.

Take Action to Re-energize
In Order to Analyze

It's impossible to even begin to assess what is happening when all your energy is gone, used up, or scattered. You must re-touch, re-center yourself by creating a space in which you can think, in which you can remove yourself temporarily from the pit. By creating mental or physical distance, you regain at least some small measure of control.

Renewing yourself can be as simple an activity as taking a long, hot shower or a bubble bath or playing the piano. Chances are, if you are imbalanced, that activity will be something in which you have not indulged recently.

Here are but a few examples of renewing activities: silence, solitude, laughter, sleep, playful reading, music, prayer, good conversation with a sharing of feelings, dancing, exercise, arts and crafts, writing, or hiking ... whatever allows you to feel at least some semblance of calm ... whatever soothes your soul without altering your ability to thoughtfully experience and reflect.

I liken this step to the Alka-Seltzer commercial— "plop, fizz, oh, what a relief it is." Notice the word is "relief," not "cure." If possible, take whatever small steps will begin to give you some control so that you might look at the bigger picture and THEN begin to change direction. For example, individuals suffering from burnout might immediately reduce at least some level of workload. One might make an appointment with a counselor or a physician.

Stage Two: Determine What Must be Acted Upon First—and Do It!

Here's another example of first-things-first: From the People Pit, Mary B. realized the first thing that had to change was her reaction to the vice president's personality and management style. Certainly depression and headaches were going nowhere and Mary knew she was definitely not coping. She also admitted that unless she could internally handle a stressful person, she'd probably continue to encounter the same problem.

Mary spent a weekend just talking and listening and talking to herself. She reevaluated her work and decided, "Darn it, I'm good." She realized that her self-confidence had been diminished by the confrontations with the vice president.

By the end of the weekend, she felt that her self-esteem was back in place and understood, finally, that the vice president was an insecure, troubled manager. With that acknowledgment, Mary knew she could internally deflect the antagonism, and knowingly play the corporate game until she had time to analyze her next move.

In this example, Mary gained personal control but did not make a major decision. However, some pits require harder efforts to gain initial control and greater space for reenergizing.

Janet E., assistant publisher.

"When I quit the magazine, I realized that it was not the work environment that had to be changed. It was me and how I reacted to it. I had been so insecure and eager to please."

Ironically, Janet began to regain her confidence when she heard Dr. Freudenberger on the *Today Show*, realized that she herself had burnout, and queried *Parade* magazine about a feature article on the topic.

"When the check came from *Parade* for $1,500, I felt my writing was validated. It took two years and lots of paid writing assignments to convince myself I was competent.

"I went back to the magazine. Only this time, I came feeling like a winner. A mediator got us together and I was able to structure the job I wished. I don't manage so many people, I work more realistic hours, and I get the salary I want. I also knew that the publisher would probably never change and read my work. So, in order to receive some of her enthusiasm and recognition, I now keep the tally of the sales records and present that to her each month."

From her two-year hiatus, Janet also was able to give up the feeling that she had to be perfect and always in control. "There's no more holding things inside. At work, when something is wrong, I now say, 'There's a problem, let's fix it.' I just love what I'm doing!"

In Janet's case, her break with work allowed a fixing-up so that she could return to the job she loved. In other instances, a break to re-energize seems to be required first for mental health and second for exploration. George G. felt he was on the brink of collapse when he left his company. Ronda S. took a one-year sabbatical to regain her sense of balance.

⚜

Sean F., professional photographer.

Having worked as a freelance photographer and photojournalist, Sean returned to school to study video productions. "I got hired by ABC and traveled the world as a cameraman for hard news. I saw the seamy, violent side of life; people killed for no reason. When I came back from these assignments,

I resigned voluntarily. I didn't want to pick up a camera again. I took a year off, not to figure out what to do with my life, but to regain my health. My value system underwent an entire re-analysis."

While few of us will ever be in Sean's position, the point is made here that sometimes our first action step might be a decision in which we feel compelled to remove ourselves ... but that's the only decision we make. The direction remains uncertain.

⁂

Gary R., former executive in the recording industry.

Although admittedly miserable in his work for some time, Gary's first action to take control of the situation finally came during an annual international meeting in Greece which he organized for the company.

"I was very uptight and uneasy during the convention. There was unnecessary pressure created from top management. You could feel the anxiety. It was created, excuse the term, by nothing more than corporate bullshit. The day after the convention broke, we had a meeting to discuss the next year's strategy. From experience, I knew that everything we said there and all the volumes of notes would never take place. What bullshit! It was an exercise in futility.

"I remember leaving that room and feeling that way. Outwardly, everyone patting each other on the back, but it was all phony."

He went to his hotel room, put on his running clothes, and told his wife not to ask any questions. "I told her I was going out and when I came back—

no matter how long it took—things would be different."

Around the city of Athens he ran. Faster. Harder. Longer. "Between the meeting, the nonsense, and the running, I knew I didn't need it any more. I didn't like the politics. I felt above what was happening. I was watching them playing a game and I didn't want to be one of the players. Everybody had this deck of cards and they were dishing them out. But no matter how often they were shuffled, you always got the same hand. I didn't want to play anymore."

When he returned to the States, Gary knew he was leaving. "I didn't know the exact date, I didn't know what I was going to do, but I knew I was leaving. Fellow employees would see me grinning and they'd ask, 'What's with you, happy face?' I'd tell them, 'I'm in a new place. Just accept it. I'm in a new place.'"

Stage Three: Begin Active Exploration

Regardless of what first step you take to regain some sense of control—whether saying "no" to another assignment or asking for a sabbatical—exploration of potential actions is now required.

This chapter contains possible exploration methods which others have found helpful in creating changes within their work or job. But remember, work is only part of the picture. In the next chapter, we'll examine "living" and the balance of both.

Dependent upon the depth of the "pit" and the possible causes, the exploration process will vary in both complexity and length of time. However, all exploration must include both external measures as well as internal dialogue. Your happiness and sense of living is a reality you first create from the inside.

Talk About Your Feelings and Possible Solutions

This is not a call for en masse gripe sessions or circular conversations that only reinforce how miserable you are. Instead, the object behind this step is to get a different perspective by receiving feedback and fresh insight from someone outside your situation. It also allows you to verbally "try out" possible actions and see how you feel about them.

Samantha "Sam" E. (fictitious name), loan officer, suburban bank.

Sam joined the bank just as the local area was being "discovered" by residents of a neighboring city. Within short order, the bank's real estate loan portfolio grew as new homes attracted newcomers to the town. Sam's manager realized that it was impossible for the department to keep up with the processing of documents and added another clerk.

Within a year, the help was still not enough. Pressure from clients mounted daily. Deadlines were critical. Sam worked overtime almost every night and still took paperwork home with her. The manager insisted that money was not available for additional help. More and more, Sam found herself dreading each day, forcing herself into the office, having no time for friends, and requiring more sleep than normal.

"I didn't mind pressure. I've always worked hard. But at least at the end of the day it was over. But now, I'm tired down to my bones."

As a first action, she talked herself into leaving work on her desk and spent a weekend at her mountain cabin. When she returned to town, Sam contacted a former associate and friend who understood the banking business.

"I shared how I felt and he gave me feedback which I hadn't considered before. By talking about my feelings I realized that I didn't want to leave my job but that I was tremendously out of balance. He provided me with some thoughts on how I might approach my boss and also validated my tentative decision not to work overtime anymore. I think I needed to hear that so I could, in fact, give myself permission to slow down. My soul is worth more than making additional money for the bank."

She also met with a stress consultant to understand just how she could change some of her work habits. "I had added to my dilemma because I didn't speak out when things became too much for me to handle."

Because Sam basically liked her chosen work, this exploration step required primarily the presence of a wisely chosen listener selected for his/her ability to provide honest, unbiased feedback. But for the deeper pits, the more severe symptoms, exploration might require professional help.

Seek Help With Work/Job Decisions— and Read

In exploring potential changes that will promote balance in our lives and a sense of control in our work/job, there are two areas that might require some outside professional assistance. The most obvious one is in the assessment of our talents, abilities, and possible career choices.

The growing interest in career management has produced numerous excellent books and countless consulting firms which many people have found helpful, if not essential, to the process of finding their true "work." Herein lies my dilemma: How do I explore this step with you in the most meaningful way?

I, too, turned to others for assistance.

Certainly in the literary marketplace Richard Bolles, author of *What Color is Your Parachute?* is the grand guru of job search and career movement. My conversations, interviews, and gut-level feeling agree that probably no single book or author has been so universally read (and followed) as Bolles. There are also others listed in the back of this book.

One might also consider a career management firm. But first, the following guidelines might be helpful:

- A contract that states exactly what you will be getting for your money.
- A program that enables you to take control of the job search process and use it many times during your life.
- A logically structured and sequenced program that is broken down into doable steps that build on each other.

- A complete program that addresses the issue of career choice as well as sound job-hunting techniques.
- A flexible, personalized program that addresses your individual needs.
- Qualified counselors who understand adult development and the career management process.

When And/Or Why Might Someone Consider Such Professional Help In The Exploration Process?

Oftentimes, exploring on your own is a problem in that you get lost, rejected, or stuck. Working through a process together keeps you rolling and doing something. It's also the old forest-for-the-trees dilemma. A good career management firm helps the client look at issues in the environment, but most of all, at skills. There is no such thing as job security, only skill. And one can learn the skill of exploration. After all, there is also no such thing as the permanent job. The process will be needed again.

What Advice Can You Give To Help The Exploration Process?

The exploration process does not necessarily mean you will change direction. Rather, the process could very well help you articulate what you need in the present situation.

According to one career consultant, "Being able to say

what you want is highly important. For example, a re-entry woman in industrial sales had three things that contributed to her 'pit': a poor boss, no opportunity to interact with others, and a car for an office. We had her attend meetings with other salespeople, where she found that her job was better than most for that line of work. We coached her so that she could talk with her boss in a nondefensive manner. She then joined professional groups and organized her time and her car better so that her environment improved."

It is equally important to maintain momentum during exploration. Keep talking, keep working, but always doing something. Inertia is everyone's greatest enemy in a process like this. Write one letter, make one phone call, attend one class, but *move*. Otherwise, you'll start a downward spiral.

Finally, be thinking about these variables in the exploration process: the work environment, roles, skills, values, and interest issues. Under work environment, consider what physical surroundings, what size organization, and what emotional tones are important to you. Do you prefer to work with people, ideas, or things? In considering your role, ask yourself in what *way* do you wish to interact with others: as a manager, a resource of information, a promoter, etc.

When it comes to skills which can be transferred from one job to another, look at more than just measurable, technical ability. There are personal skills (stick-to-it-ness, analytical or creative ability, honesty, etc.) as well as skills in planning, writing, organizing, speaking, and others. Remember, the skills that come naturally, easily, and are most enjoyable are the ones you really prefer. The more those preferred skills are utilized, the more energized and challenged you will be.

Lastly, look at interest issues—those bigger-than-myself causes that capture your emotions and passions, such as the environment, abused children, human rights, hunger. Like preferred skills, if there are such interest issues in your life, you will be more energized if your work deals with these issues.

Seek Help With Life Context

The second area which might require a new look and professional assistance is self-discovery. The understanding of who we are in relation to everything else can very well make a difference in the work and balance choices we make as well as our attitude toward those choices.

To explain, I'd like you to think about a snowflake. We know that each snowflake is different. In fact, let's assume that there will never be another snowflake like the one that is right now drifting to earth.

As the snowflake dances on the winter air, it behaves just like a snowflake should, bowing and dipping in turn with its other snowflakes. Once upon the ground, the snowflake becomes part of a snowdrift. As the wind whistles and the temperature drops, the flakes press tighter against each other.

Our snowflake keeps its identity, but the context in which it must now operate is different. Not only is it no longer alone but there is a different response needed to the current situation. In the winter's dance, Little Snowflake could spin lightly around, showing off whatever dancing talent it had. Now, its talents are called upon to bear the weight of other snowflakes, to respond in a different fashion.

The analogy could continue with the snowflake changing into a drop of water that sits in a mud puddle, is evaporated and becomes a cloud, later returning to earth as rain. In all these instances, the context changes under which Little Snowflake lives, and moves, and has its being.

The same concept applies to humans. By looking at the movement of our life and the context in which we interact with others, we begin to realize the *continuity* and *purpose* and *meaning* which we bring to each day.

Perhaps this concept is easier to understand if I share Robert Wendorf's insight. After all, it is based upon his personal experience with life context that Robert discontinued his Beverly Hills practice and moved to a slower-paced city where he could concentrate on these issues with clients.

⚜

Robert W., psychotherapist.

"My journey through 'the pits' wasn't confined to any one time. It was rather a period of experiencing some things that were very foreign to me. I began exploring yoga with a teacher from India. ... meeting people who were putting higher and higher priorities on their health, worship, exercise, and things that I had always considered secondary.

"A shift was taking place in who I was. It was agony and ecstasy. Painful. Exciting. Frightening. Questioning. There was no single turning point but rather a series. One turning point was seeing that I had the practice I had long since sought, that I was making good money, that I could play the game, that I had invested a lot of money in personal therapy, and still something was missing."

He added a side note that clinicians either confront their own anxieties with therapy, leave the field or move into administration.

"What I was discovering was that I was truly a

part of the process of *life*. That *life* is expressing itself through me. This was something new to me.

"When I was counseled by other professionals, no one dealt with a change in context. No one ever said 'who are you?' It is necessary to know that I am part of a bigger picture, that I go through periods of doubt and confusion but that nevertheless life is unfolding in me. I have value! *This* was what was missing for me. You must hear it over and over again before it becomes integrated.

"This is what I do in my psychotherapy and transition counseling. I assist people in understanding and experiencing themselves as a unique part of the overall process of life."

※

Robert is not a lone voice crying from a mountain top. Now there are counselors and therapists who guide individuals in understanding the movement of their lives.

Other avenues of life-context exploration are available through workshops designed by people like Robert.

There is value in all of them, even if deciding which to attend is difficult. Since we respond differently to certain formats, personalities, and methods of presentation, it might take several attempts before you find a workshop that strikes a personal chord. But it is well worth the effort.

For me, I have found tremendous value in the Intensive Journal Workshop. Designed in 1966 by Dr. Ira Progoff, a New York psychologist, student of Carl Jung, and a founder of the Association for Humanistic Psychology, this journal method provides a lifelong tool for making life more whole and integrated. Or as *Psychology Today* (March 1981) reported, "Not a therapist, not a guru, but a philosopher psychologist who follows Tillich, Buber, and Jung, Ira Progoff teaches journal keeping as a way to help focus one's life."

Now administered by Dialogue House in New York, the Intensive Journal program has been taught to some 50,000 participants around the world, in colleges, branches of the armed forces, hospitals, prisons, and churches. The Intensive Journal process provides a systematic yet individualized and private approach for clarifying where you are now in your life, determining what resources are present, and deciding on new directions. No, you don't have to be a writer to use it and no, you don't write in it every day. But as the need arises, I have found myself perched on my bed or sitting on the beach with my journal in hand, watching feelings and connections flow—without judgment or censorship—from my pen. Amazing what I discover! But remember, this method is what I have decided works for me. Your choices are, and must be, uniquely patterned to you.

Certainly help of this nature might not take priority among the action steps required for your immediate situation, but my heart (as well as my research) insists that I include this step. To paraphrase Socrates: "The unexamined life is a life not worth living."

Take Exploratory Courses

A corresponding reason for the depression and helplessness experienced when work/job is out of balance, is that options appear limited. A way to alter that perception is by examining other fields of interest which have been ignored or forgotten. There is tremendous power in knowledge.

In trying to work her way through the "pit" as director of communication, Cheryl P. enrolled in a fiction class. Her limited on-the-job writing was then expanded by this extracurricular activity. To her surprise, she discovered that she relished each course assignment and the desire to write became even stronger.

By the end of the first day in a course entitled, "Career Transitions for Educators, "Ronda S. decided to request a leave of absence. "In the workshop, I started to believe I had other strengths. Maybe I *did* have other things that I could do!"

Charles D. learned the same thing. Even before leaving his $6 million corporation, he had started taking night classes in psychology. "After I quit, I went to Europe for my first vacation in ten years. I came home with the realization that I didn't want to be a marketing executive. The psychology course had touched an old but never satisfied interest. I entered college as a full-time student to earn a M.A. in counseling."

Not all exploratory classes open doors.

Loan Officer Samantha, in trying to evaluate potential solutions for her out-of-balance situation, decided to take a course in surveying. "I had a real estate background before coming to the bank and I was getting more involved in that field with the type of loan documents I was handling. Since I also liked being outdoors, the thought of land surveying seemed appealing."

She took the course and found the practical work to be dull and uninteresting. "But I felt better. It was just as important to look at that area and then decide I didn't want it."

Practice Networking

With or without professional help, the results of the exploration process can explode tenfold by utilizing networking. A network is an information web, the process of equalizing opportunity by sharing knowledge. One reaches out to others, researches and learns through the sharing of experiences, broadens contacts, and gains a wider view of the world than before.

Charles D., now counselor and video producer.
"I knew the home improvement industry inside and out when I left. But I had blinders on to the rest of the world. I didn't know much about such things as consultants, colleges, and cable video programs. So I made a decision to grow."

He cut his ties with the industry and instead made a goal to meet two new interesting people a week. "Authors, athletes, someone written up in the paper, whoever intrigues me …I called and asked them to lunch. Without knowing it, I began creating a network."

Ronda S., now sales representative for education equipment company.
Networking became a way of life for Ronda when she took her leave of absence and moved to the same city as her boyfriend. Prior to leaving the school, she sent a note to her friends and colleagues, asking for the names and addresses of anyone they knew in her new town who might be a general connection.

"Armed with that list, I contacted these somewhat-new 'friends.' At first, my concept in meeting people had been you-are-what-you-work. Since I no longer had work, with these folks I practiced getting out and saying what my skills were. Not only was I practicing getting out there and informally investigating, but I was learning to convince others that I could do something besides teach."

She also began collecting information through corporate interview—not asking for a job, but merely seeking information about specific industries. Additionally, by attending the meetings of a wide variety of professional associations which encouraged guests, she was able to expand her circle of acquaintances and her potential work ideas.

"I also spoke with educators who had made a transition, asking them what had been most successful for them. Some even let me sit in on their job and observe if I thought I might be interested in that occupation.

"I'd even go talk with employment agencies, if for no other reason than to practice talking about my skills. That way, I became even clearer in my own mind what my potential really was."

⚜

Simple informational networking also empowers by expanding personal horizons. In a conversation with Jennifer, a successful bank manager, I discovered she'd been an art major who entered banking because a divorce settlement forced her to support a family. "So I guess I'll just have to stay here," she sighed. "I don't know anything else to do."

She was subsequently astonished to consider that there might be ways to blend her love of art with her financial background: as an art appraiser and consultant, a consultant on corporate art collections, a buyer for galleries, etc.

"Why, I never thought of such things," she exclaimed.

She also had never considered looking beyond the obvious. Informational networking might have opened new vistas.

Surround Yourself With Positive People

The exploration process is difficult enough without negative feedback from the outside. As Mark Twain so aptly insisted, "Keep away from people who belittle your ambitions. Small people try to do that, but really great people make you feel that you, too, can become great."

The search for the work of our lives and attendant balance requires us to travel through peaks and valleys. Develop a support network of individuals who will encourage you, who might even be going through the same process so that you no longer feel alone. One career counseling firm feels so strongly about this that they gather their clients together at a weekly informal party for the sole purpose of sharing ups and downs.

Use Both Sides of Your Brain

There's a tendency to reduce our exploration to the logical, head-felt actions. Period. But we are also people of emotions, creativity (no matter how stifled), and feelings. In fact, no matter how analytical you might be in the present out-of-balance "pit," the rock-bottom reality is that you do not *feel* happy. Period.

To get in touch with those feelings as well as to affirm your own growth process, try success imaging. Cut out magazine pictures of people who show how you'd like to feel, what you'd like to be doing. At night, think of yourself in a place of balance, control and energy. Feel what it is like to be there. In fact, as you explore alternative changes in direction, *feel* (not think about) how it would be if such a change were to occur.

From personal experience, I know that more than one choice has been altered because it just didn't *feel* right. We have a lot more power in both hemispheres of our brain than we give credit to.

Reward Yourself
Each Time You Stretch

Why is it that we think of rewarding children when they have performed in an exceptional manner (for their specific ability) but forget to reward ourselves for doing something that requires extra efforts? That's what stretching is—doing something which we find hard to do. It might be writing a letter, talking to a counselor, reading an article, discussing how we feel, even pushing to get to an exercise class because instinctively you know your body needs to be renewed.

Whatever it is, Ronda S. shares a way of accounting and rewarding these stretches. "To influence my behavior, I pick out something that I know I should do but don't. Then, each time I do it, I put a sticker on the calendar. Four stickers and I acknowledge myself: getting my nails done, going to the theater, anything that rewards my effort."

Be Patient and Flexible

The decision-making process does not happen overnight. There are many avenues to explore, tentative action steps to consider. A choice is a process, not an end result. As you learn more about yourself, the choices will change. Rigid decisions are like icicles—brittle, stiff, cold, and subject to shattering or melting. A flexible posture within this process, however, allows you to unfold like a sailboat spinnaker to capture all the wind. However, flexible does not mean that you never make a choice; that you vacillate like a will-o'-wisp and therefore never move forward.

In summary, at this point in the process, you have made no decisions other than to analyze, re-energize, take whatever immediate step is called for to gain some small measure of control, and to explore. There are still other parts of you—the other components that make up living—that need to be considered.

Summary

1. Stage One: Analysis of the situation. Accept responsibility for your role in the pit
   - Look at attitudes
   - Look at your response to personal history
   - Look at your response to social pressure
   - Determine the level of expectation
   - Determine if the "pit" is *really* work/job or a cover-up

      –   Take action to re-energize

2. Stage Two: Determine the first action and do it

3. Stage Three: Begin active exploration

      –   Talk about your feelings and
          possible solutions

      –   Seek help with work/job decisions
          and analysis

      –   Seek help in understanding life context

      –   Take exploratory courses

      –   Practice networking

      –   Surround yourself with positive people

      –   Use both sides of your brain

      –   Reward yourself for stretching

      –   Be patient and flexible

Chapter Five

This Thing Called "Live"

What would you say if I asked you, "tell me what it means to be fully alive?" Thanks to the graciousness of author John Powell, S.J., I recently taught a one-day intro-duction session to his *Fully Alive Experience* and asked that very question of participants. I divided them into groups, handed them a sheet of newsprint, and said, "go to it."

Within fifteen minutes, after much laughter, the results were posted around the room: eating all the ice cream you want, going to the theater, backpacking, hugging the family, driving with the top down, telling jokes, solving problems, loving without expecting, bubble baths, experiencing the full range of feelings, and on and on.

Of the twenty-eight people present, no one said anything about working.

Why is it that we think working and living are mutually exclusive?

Counterpoint: If I had asked the participants, "what does success mean?" I'd be willing to bet that the majority of the responses would not include any of the "fully alive" activities.

To be fair to the wonderful people gathered on that spring Saturday morning, I think the group might have eventually come up with some correlation. But not at first. We are conditioned to think of success first in terms of achievement, fame, and fortune.

Notice these three words: achievement, fame, fortune. They are words of quantity, of more and most; recognizable symbols to the outside world. But they may not mean quality.

The truth is that there is as much "success" in catching a trout, comforting a friend, or kneeling before whatever Higher Power you profess, as there is in making a killing on Wall Street, heading up a corporation, or closing a crucial sale.

The truth is that there can be just as much "aliveness" in designing a car, teaching a class, or developing a marketing campaign as there is in skinny-dipping, lobster dinners, and naps in a hammock.

What throws us askew and out of the hammock, into an either-or-posture, is a continual lack of balance. And we get that way by the choices we make—with our work/job choice as the cornerstone. Let me first expand on what I mean by balance.

The Meaning Of Balance

Balance is really interconnectedness. If I could draw you a picture, it would have five circles joined together: intellectual stimulus (our work/job), material possessions (money and "things"), emotional stability (love), physical well-being, and spiritual wholeness.

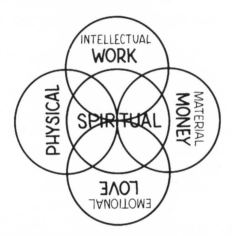

If the circles are not all connected, something is missing. The miracle of human existence is that we *are* multifaceted; that our integration of who we are comes from touching *all* the various parts of us. If in our picture of living we leave even one circle untouched or if one is so big that it overshadows the others, then the quality of life diminishes.

Thanks to the media, we are privy to the tragic tales of some public figures who, by the first standards of success, had it "made." In reality, many had lost touch with essential parts of life: with love, physical well-being, spiritual wholeness. Where was the quality of life for Howard Hughes or Marilyn Monroe?

Yes, these are sensational, dramatic cases. We shake our heads, mutter "poor souls," and then often continue down the same (though less public) road—more often than not in pursuit of our own modified version of fame and fortune. Winston Churchill said it best: "Men occasionally stumble over the truth, but most of them pick themselves up and hurry off, as if nothing had happened."

Case in point: I had been invited to attend a meeting with a gentleman who, according to his definition and those around him, was a "success" because he was paid some well-above average fee for his speeches and seminars. "Okay," I thought. "Sounds fine so far."

Throughout the dinner, he told me how he plotted marketing strategy, how many phone calls he made a day, how he spent weekends (he's not married) making contacts for business development. "I'll be one of the most successful, high paid speakers on the circuit."

A very talented musician closed the evening. His final number, which brought down the house, as well as tears to many eyes, was a song he had written about his friend, a handicapped child. "Wow," I said, wiping my eyes. "What did you think of that song?" The middle-aged gentleman turned to me with a puzzled look,

"Oh, I didn't pay any attention to that. I was making notes about some of his stage techniques which I might use."

His response saddened me. Single-minded attention to being a success had lost him a powerful, magical experience.

Don't get me wrong. Ambition, a desire to be recognized for our efforts, and hard work are all admirable qualities. But it's the over-concentration for extended periods of time—in any of the five areas—that distorts the picture, disconnects us, creates imbalance.

Balance also implies that one knows when one of the circles should be made larger—and it's generally the one that has been getting fainter and fainter from lack of touching.

A colleague observed to me, "Businessmen and women today are the world's greatest jugglers. They juggle enormous job responsibilities, financial demands, community involvement, spousal needs, parenting chores, social commitments and more. It often seems that they are being pulled apart—that everybody is taking a piece of them—until there is nothing left for themselves."

More and more it is becoming clear that for the executive and professional, there is really no definite separation between one's personal and business life. They are tremendously and significantly interwoven. It is just as important to manage the business of your life as it is to manage the life of your business.

True balance is not an equality but rather an active, conscious connection to the integral parts of our life. Nor is it a static condition. When balance is defined as "connection," the metaphor for our journey becomes sailing.

In a single-person boat, you have one hand on the tiller, one on the sheet, and if the wind is strong and the boat is diving into the water at a steep pitch, your feet are also hooked under the railing. At this point, the boat looks out of balance. What keeps it moving forward, however, is that you are consciously connected to all the critical parts of that boat. As the wind changes or as you decide to alter direction, your connection with the integral parts will change.

So too in life. Depending upon the shift of the wind, where you want to go, and the weight you are carrying, the sails must be trimmed, let out, maybe even hauled in. The

crucial point is that we all learn how to sail. We can stay on
a hard tack when necessary, but we can also come about and
head for a sheltered port, connected at all times to every part
of our life.

Finally, balance is not a static condition. Throughout
the rest of the book, you'll be able to observe the "sailing"
techniques of others, the choices made to remain connected,
and also the choices that sadly created imbalance and a life
of probable quantity but not quality.

Circle #1: Intellectual Stimulus of Work/Job

Since it is the source of self-definition and that which
energizes and utilizes our own special talents and preferred
skills, finding the "work" of our lives remains a primary
task. To qualify as your "piece of work," it will also be
something which you can point to or speak about and say,
"There—I did it!" But don't think the "work" needs to be
earth-shattering. It is just as important, if not more so, to be
the faithful brick in the foundation as it is to be the
capstone.

However, the choices we make about our "work" or
"job" act upon every corner of our life and vice-versa. That's
why it makes the most sense to look at the full picture of
just what creates a quality life before moving further.

Rohrlich calls work a "state of mind," and I would
have to agree. As you go through the exploratory process,
you'll find that the areas which excite you are those to
which you can freely give your concentration. Hopefully, at
the same time, you are also discovering your own giftedness.

I bring up this idea of "giftedness" so that you might have a different perspective on the circle called "intellectual stimulus."

I purposely have not yet spoken about money in relation to your work choice because that confines your thinking. Unlike the typical "success" career seminars which start off by asking you "What do you want to make?" I'd rather ask you, "Who do you want to be?" "How do you want to feel?"

⚜

John B., Ph.D., Industrial Psychologist.

Even as a teenager, John always opted for learning. "When I worked during high school, my parents had a hard time understanding why I would leave a $5/hour job at the local grocery to intern for half the pay with the PR director for United Way. But I knew why; he said he would teach me how to write." The lure of constant learning, as well as his special giftedness for teaching, led to the doctorate and also a highly lucrative consulting position with one of the nation's largest consulting firms.

"Everyone thought I was crazy when I left the firm after they had made an extremely attractive offer. They thought I was even crazier to leave it for a teaching position at a technical college. But I knew that what I was doing was saner for me."

He purposely selected a college which would also allow him to maintain a private consulting practice and which did not hold to the doctrine of "publish or perish."

"My outside work helps me to be an excellent teacher because I can bring the real world into the classroom. With my consulting practice, I have

traveled around the world on challenging assignments, returned to the security and the constant
variety of teaching, and taken sabbaticals for additional study as well as quality time with my wife. In
fact, I just turned down more consulting work with
my largest client because I want to write and spend
more time with Barbara."

⊰ৡৠৡ⊱

Do you see how John's choices to follow his special
giftedness have, in turn, allowed him to remain connected
to other parts of his life? His work is not selected for its
traditional "success" value.

By the same token, giftedness can also be overused to
a point where life becomes bitter and stale because of
single-minded devotion to work rather than to living.

Circle #2: Material Possessions— Money

Like Tweedledum and Tweedledee, the roly-poly,
always-fighting twins from *Alice in Wonderland,* choices
for material possessions/money and work/job go hand in
hand. And frequently in conflict.

For example, we've already noticed that if work
success is equated strictly with money, options for growing
and living are influenced solely by an arbitrary job market
and *not* by one's own giftedness.

⊰ৡৠৡ⊱

*George G. (fictitious name), recently retired
senior executive with multinational corporation.*
"I sold myself to the devil because it paid a hell

of a lot more money," George explained when asked why he returned to the corporation which he had left ten years earlier.

"I had gone through a divorce; my public relations firm was not successful; I had spent two years in analysis; and my financial accumulation had decreased. And I was just a few years from retirement."

Now retired, George is still not a happy man. He can't bring himself to really try what might be one of his true gifts, cartooning. "The bitch goddess of success is always there. Certainly using myself as a dictionary, it's most often tied up with monetary things. You've got to be a success every minute or you're a failure. My goal now is to get over the fear of failure."

⚜

There are other subtle voices that creep into our subconscious and stifle our ability to assert the power of choice. Have you heard any of these lately:
- I went without—my child won't!
- We'll be much happier if we have more money and don't fight over the bills.
- I must have money in the bank for rainy days.

If you listen to voice number one, consider this: I doubt there's a child psychologist around who would tell you to give a youngster "things" first and *then* love. If in doing your job or "work," you're unhappy or spend little quality time at home, I sincerely doubt that making up for your "lost" childhood is filling up an empty spot in a young heart. And maybe, just maybe, using the child's welfare as a "reason" might be a coverup for another voice that says, "I'll show them (people from the past)!"

Arguments over money, as indicated by voice number two, are the second most common causes of fights between couples. But there's often more to it than what meets the ear. As a communications consultant, effective listening is one of the skills which I teach. All too frequently, what is spoken is not what is really said. Behind the verbalized arguments about money could be deeper messages:

- I'm angry at you for ignoring me.
- If I buy you things, then you'll love me.
- I don't know how to express my feelings.
- I really want to have some meaningful work of my own. This will force the issue.

Lastly is the idea that money buys security. Yes and no. It gives the impression of security. But what does that mean when you've lost everything in a tornado? If your business fails and you declare bankruptcy? The *only* security is yourself. That's where the strength is; that's what you can count on. When all else fails, you—little ol' you—are the winning card.

What value, then, are you if in the push for security you've damaged your health, your happiness, maybe even denied your true talents?

Do you see how these attitudes, if played to the hilt, limit your freedom to truly live?

Money And Personal Ability

While admitting that self-worth comes from our internal view of ourselves, it is also absolutely true that money is an indication of just what others think of our efforts. The better someone is at what they do, the financial reward should reflect that ability.

Do you see the difference, the balance, within this

type of approach to monetary gain? Try this thought process on for size: "Pay me not because I'm a failure without it or that I need the security, but because I'm good at what I do."

I personally think the issue of money as a reflection of ability is why many gifted teachers leave the public school system.

One former teacher explained it this way, "The principal told me I was a good manager so I always ended up with the problem kids. I worked hard and could take care of them but it didn't seem fair to be paid the same as teachers with lighter loads and easier classes."

Material Possessions and Impact on Work Choice

One day at the local hardware store, a gardener for one of the wealthy estates on Long Island ran into a friend whom he hadn't seen in some time. "Say," said the friend, "I understand you're working for that banker now."

"Nope, you've got it all wrong," responded the gardener. "Why, each morning he's up at 4:30, rides that stuffy train into the city, stays there until late at night, and then comes home bleary eyed just so he can keep up his estate and pay me my weekly wages. Nope, the way I see it, he's working for me!"

Sometimes, our choices of material possessions or a lifestyle become the dragon that we end up feeding with our very happiness.

∘⁣ᕷ⁣∘

Joe S., Senior executive in entertainment conglomerate.

"I hate what I do. People drive me crazy but they

_._.-

pay me a bloody fortune. I've got a lifestyle to keep
up. I can't go back to being poor. My kids have to be
in private school. I love fine restaurants and golf. I
do all this to feed the lifestyle. I'm as happy as I
could be working."

⚜

Most people aren't as honest as this unhappy
executive. Instead, what I have more commonly heard is
this remark of discontent, "They pay me too much money to
quit." The truth is that such people have made choices for a
lifestyle which now has claimed power over their very lives.
(That power can be wrested away, but not without difficulty.)

Notice, too, the latter person's inability to accept
responsibility: "they" are to blame.

Sure we all have that basic nut to crack. And sometimes, to get the things in our lives that we want, we will
make a choice for money and material goods. But not to the
point where we lose control of the hypothetical sailboat and
plunge into turbulent water with diamonds, cars, trips, and
mansions flailing against the mast.

The trick to staying in balance seems to be in
acknowledging just why you are making the choice and in
staying connected in other areas.

Some months ago while I was working on a pothole of
a project at 3:30 a.m., I finally met the office janitor. I
learned that this young man, father of two, was employed in
a series of jobs so that he could put a good-sized down-
payment on a house for his growing family. "The kids really
love it there. Good family spot."

I also discovered that his series of cleaning jobs began
at midnight and his full-time maintenance work started in
the morning. But his latter job also afforded him flexibility

to take time off so he could attend daytime school functions with his youngsters.

Yet for all that work, he stood grinning at me in that ungodly morning hour. He didn't feel trapped or abused by the need to work long hours for the new home. By a conscious choice, plus an apparent effort to remain in touch with other areas of his life, he apparently remained in control.

In this next example, working extra hours to maintain a home only caused additional stress and imbalance.

⚜

Sandy R., former elementary school teacher, now a traveling sales rep for the mechanical power division of a Fortune 500 company.

"Not only was there no justice in the fact that I was carrying heavier loads, always working well past the regular hours, and not getting paid for it, but reality started to sink in. I gave up my idea of Prince Charming coming along. Being thirty-four and single, I had to work two jobs to buy a home. Instead of vacations, I worked. It was just too much.

"When I started training for this job, I was paid $1,000 more for knowing nothing more than I did when I left teaching! I'll never go back as long as money is an issue."

⚜

For other people, getting rid of a possession is a way to regain a sense of "living" … even if only for a while.

⚜

Timothy C., (fictitious name) dean of faculty for a Christian college

He had been an urban dweller all his life: twenty years in New York and sixteen years in San

Francisco. But for the past four years, this man and his family gave up all attachments which created a burden and limited their freedom of choice. They sold the home, moved to the mountains, lived in a trailer and even in a Buddhist community while he commuted to work. They've returned now to the city for the dearly missed theaters, libraries, and variety of people. But with a difference. "We're renting now. I'll never own a home again."

※

Just as material choices impact other areas, so too might work choices impact the material. Accept a certain job and you might have to join a club in order to entertain. You might need a larger car to carry samples. Nothing new about these alterations in living. I remember my dad doing them. What *is* relatively new within the movement toward finding the "work" of one's life, one's giftedness and happiness, is that work choices might now require a "giving up" of material things.

※

Gary R., now president of R & R Management Associates.

With the decision to leave the trade magazine, Gary began the exploration process. He discovered that his prior experience in putting on meetings for the corporation was something that not only pleased him but which, from conversations with others, was indeed a form of "giftedness." But starting a business as a meeting planning consultant from a home office, without the weekly paycheck, meant adjustment for everyone.

The annual family vacation to Europe became a quick trip to Catalina Island. Expensive restaurants were replaced with two-for-one dinners. His wife Geri still drives a ten-year-old Buick that keeps hanging in there, and the redecorating and painting of the home will just have to wait.

Although Geri had already started a part-time sales job at a local department store prior to Gary's departure from the company, she's now counted on to carry the family on her employee medical insurance policy.

"I figured that we had enough to live on for two years—if we lived frugally. But this is going to work. I just know it."

In looking at what we want in our life, in performing the work that satisfies, we might find great freedom in the idea of simplistic living or "thinking in minimums." If we wait until we have all we want before we do what we want, the opportunity could vanish.

You can only sleep on one set of sheets at a time, eat from one dish, sit in one room. I realized this when I came to California with whatever would fit in a Camaro and a new life ready to be filled. There's tremendous freedom in knowing what you need. The rest of the wants you can go after, but without attachment.

As for what you might need—an individual preference, to be sure—I'm partial to this thought: "If you have but pennies left, forget bread and buy hyacinths to feed your soul."

Circle #3: Emotional Stability—Love

According to Sigmund Freud, work and love are the basic requirements of human existence. Although doubt has been raised on other proclamations from this father of modern psychotherapy, his statement about work and love appears more firmly grounded.

In fact, the length of our very life seems to be influenced by whether or not we have a significant love relationship! It is one of the factors in determining probable longevity and also the quality of life. Dr. George Vallaint, found that the single most powerful indicator of later life contentment was neither income nor career success. Rather, the existence of positive, happy family relations was the key to "living."

However, decisions and attitudes about work frequently impact the presence, quantity, and quality of love. In some cases, it might really be the primary cause for a "pit."

"Sometimes, the real problem is not the work but that these high-powered men and women need someone in their life. They've traveled, made a lot of money, but have never nested ... been a husband, wife, or parent. And that's what's lacking," stated a human resource executive.

But more commonly, the work impacts an already present relationship.

In the '80s the Silicon Valley, was California's hottest gold-rush site, where overnight fortunes in electronics flashed at the zap of a microchip. Home of one-thousand-plus high-tech companies, the area had been portrayed as the epitome of free enterprise and prosperity.

However, according to Judith Larsen and Carol Gill of Cognos Associates, a non-profit research center in Los

Altos, the Silicon Valley image tarnished. In a study titled, "Changing Lifestyle in Silicon Valley," they wrote, "The Silicon Valley myth was a dream.... The long hours and constant pressure wore away at individuals. Perhaps the most profound impact was the deterioration of the interpersonal relationships—marriage and family."

Therapists and law enforcement officials said there were growing signs that this high-pressure, competitive environment was taking a large toll on divorce, child abuse, alcoholism, and drug use. At the time of the study, the divorce rate was higher than the rate for California as a whole, and California's rate was 20 percent above the U. S. average.

Through the microcosm of Silicon Valley, we see a magnified view of the modern dilemma which is present everywhere. Dr. Jay B. Rohrlich, author of *Work and Love: The Crucial Balance,* used his psychiatric practice on Wall Street as a resource for his groundbreaking book. His conclusion: What it takes to succeed in work is precisely the opposite of what is required for success in love. Work is a manipulation of materials, ideas, or people to achieve an end result. Love is "being with" and that "being with" cannot be measured, defined, or result in an "I did it!" statement.

Hopefully, by understanding this dilemma which Rohrlich so skillfully presents and which I have condensed tremendously, one can begin to make conscious choices to achieve this delicate balance. Such choices could entail everything from modification of working habits (possibly with help through counseling) to major shifts in lifestyle or work.

Back in 1983, Bjorn Borg astounded the tennis professionals by deciding to leave his career for—*love!* As *Time* magazine announced "During this holiday, Borg unexpectedly found out how pleasant life was without tennis. Along with his wife of two-and-one-half years ... he lapsed into the most debilitating state of all, contentment."

While I questioned (and rightfully so) the wisdom of totally renouncing a career that obviously used his amazing talents, many examples abound of people who have made a significant work decision in favor of a relationship.

One high-powered young woman, up for consideration as a vice president in a highly prestigious corporation, determined that reaching such heights would only more severely curtail the ability to spend time with her very special man. "If our relationship is ever going to grow, I've got to tend it. I'm already working extended hours and many weekends. I just don't want to work harder and risk losing him. It's not worth the price."

⋘⋙

Jane J., president of an international transportation company.

Employees for Jane know there's more to the trim lovely woman with soft, gentle eyes and warm smile than one would expect. After all, they gave her the plaque which has her picture superimposed over a *Forbes* magazine cover blaring this headline: 'The Best Man For the Job'. . . .

From her rise as a clerk, packer, secretary, sales rep, and finally president, one readily believes her when she admits, "I love this company." She took it over at the age of thirty-six, with eight employees and about $1.5 million in business. Ten years later, revenue now hits the $14 million mark.

An earlier marriage had ended in divorce. For her, there was nothing else but the company. Until love changed all that. "If it wasn't for him, I'd be here day and night. We've been together fifteen years, although not married. I don't need to be married. But within the first five years, he changed and so did I. He left his yacht and million-dollar house, and said 'What's it for? All I want to do is to spend the rest of my life with you.'"

He's teaching me to let go. We need time and now I'm starting to claim it. And I'm learning that my company will be better for it. It's not easy. I do things faster and easier because I've done them for so long. But now, I know I must release the employees to be creative and to make their own mistakes. Now, I'm better than I wanted to be. I like myself a lot."

Isn't love grand? The presence of love can also impact how well you work, which in turn might impact how much money you make. I know I've grown professionally and personally because of the presence of a wonderful, unconditionally loving husband in my life. I'm happier, more enthusiastic, less tense, and more patient. Because I feel good about myself and extremely blessed, I'm more willing to risk, take chances, even leave the security of a paycheck to open my consulting practice.

Emotional stability (love) is not limited to a sexual relationship, but depends instead on the presence of others whose love draws you out of yourself and before whom you stand accepted. Choices for love therefore also include family, friends, and (particularly for members of the religious life) God. "Greater Love than this no man has."

Circle #4: Physical Well-Being

The dramatic rise of corporate recreation specialists points to the inevitable conclusion: without a healthy body, you are less productive. Although this sounds rather bottom line, you also can't be productive in love or in quality living if your body fails to respond.

Included in this area of physical well-being are exercise, nutrition, and recreation. It is not necessary to delve into the benefits of a regular exercise routine or the wisdom in cutting back on red meats, alcohol, and high cholesterol foods. One would have to be catatonic not to have read, heard, or seen the massive amount of information that is currently available on the subject.

The important point to stress again is your responsibility to touch and stay in balance with this area of life. It's not always easy. If I've had a long, hard day and time approaches for my aerobics class, there's a mighty big temptation to go home instead. If I give in and refrain from class, I have found that I am crankier, have less energy, and don't think quite as clearly.

Our bodies also serve as excellent barometers for letting us know when our proverbial sailboat is headed for rough water. If, that is, we stop long enough to notice the falling mercury and if we are willing to change direction.

These can be mighty big "ifs." Elizabeth, a human resource director for a major corporation, had to reach the point where eczema left her in agony and scarcely able to walk before she admitted that something was seriously wrong with her working and living.

"I remember becoming so angry at a leading dermatologist who told me that the eczema would stop when I was ready to listen to what it had to teach me. How right he turned out to be. For one thing, my body was screaming 'enough'. My work and the publication of a successful book had captured almost every waking minute of my life. I was truly out of balance. Second, through an est workshop I also realized that my body was replicating the picture I mentally held of myself—namely, that I was unattractive. Why would my handsome husband ever stay with me? As soon as I rebalanced my life and my thinking, the eczema began to go away!"

Physical exercise, nutrition, and recreation might also be considered work. There is tremendous concentration, something tangible is gained (I lost ten pounds, I did sixteen more push-ups, I beat Tom at tennis 40-Love) and there is a manipulation of some object. This can be carried to extremes which is probably why workaholics, if they do take time off, never seem to be rested. Recreation becomes a form of work with goals that have to be achieved.

With this thought in mind, it becomes easier to understand why we also must touch the final circle, spiritual wholeness.

Circle #5: Spiritual Wholeness

Apart from the tug and pull of intellectual, material, emotional, and physical concerns, there is a part of us that must simply "be," alone and yet at one with a Power that is above, within and around us. For some, that power has a name: Jehovah, Christ, Buddha, Allah. For others, it remains unnamed. But for all, it is vitally important to make choices which allow us the time and space to simply "be"; to reconnect our innermost being with the same wellspring of life which makes our very breathing an essential part of the Whole.

Now before you panic and think you're headed for a religion lesson, consider this: One of the things I am talking about is leisure.

Philosopher Joseph Pieper, writing in *Leisure: The Basis of Culture,* defined it best. "Leisure is a mental and spiritual attitude—not the inevitable result of spare time—*it* is an attitude of contemplative celebration.... Leisure is the power to overstep the boundaries of the workaday world and reach out ... to forces that refresh and renew us."

Leisure is not work and therefore not recreation. There is no product, no accomplishment, no win or lose. Because no "thing" is achieved, it *is*—to some ways of thinking—a waste of time.

I think it can be the most significant time. Let me give you an example.

⚜

Joanne T., organizational management consultant and now head of a kayak company.

Although a biochemist by undergraduate education, by age twenty-one she was acting as the director of management analysis for a large federal government agency. Her career had zoomed from there to consulting assignments with city agencies, major corporations and school systems.

Balance is critically important to her. Leisure, the contemplative at-one-with, carries high priority in her life.

"No matter how excited I get about my work, and this truly is my life's work, no matter how rich I feel after a successful encounter with client groups, my heart is really in the woods ... in nature. [She paused in the telling, closed her eyes, and after a minute or so, opened them. Tears glistened.] See, I can put myself there. It's where I belong, a different level of richness. It's a sacrament. Maybe that's why I take a total of twelve weeks during the course of a year and disappear—to be in the woods and to be with friends.

"Why just last week, in the middle of all the craziness of work, I took off ten hours to learn how to handle a new kayak. But to be honest, it didn't matter whether I learned it or not. I just needed to 'be.' I feel free to make those choices."

⚜

She's not alone in understanding the true meaning of leisure. The catamaran boat captain in Kona who relishes just "being" on the water, the executive who sleeps outside sometimes just to watch the stars, or the general manager of a country club who slings his backpack across his shoulders and heads into the High Sierras for two weeks have found a space for "being."

Nor does it have to be so exotic. I rise an extra hour early so that I may sit and meditate—nothing more, just "be." But it is a conscious choice that is all part of my personal picture of balance. For all of us, it is essential that we claim some personal time for just "being" with ourselves and, in my case at least, with my God.

For many, spiritual wholeness might also include more "doable" activities: reading contemplative books, affirmation cards, attendance at worship services ... whatever puts us in touch with a world that is much bigger than ourselves. Out of that world comes the context for our "work."

⚜

Robert W.

"During contemplative sessions as I struggled to understand what was happening in my career and life, I discovered that we are all part of one Force, one Being, one God. All of us are expressions of that universal energy, that Universal Being. That everything we do falls within the law of cause and effect … that it comes back to you. You become 'the other guy.' Before, my ego attempted to derive its sense of goodness from that which is Universal. I am a part of Life. Life is expressing itself through me. I am universal. How then can I be steward of talent for the Planet? It's a pretty big rearrangement. That's why I say it's a shift in the context of your life. Who you are, what you are, what you are doing and why you're doing it is now different."

⚜

Another thought for spiritual wholeness: Honoring the miracle that is uniquely "you" and touching that "you" can be difficult. The more frequent message telegraphed to us is that you do not pat yourself on the back, that you celebrate others but not yourself. Concentrate on what is wrong with you rather than what is right.

Joanne offered a suggestion for countering these tendencies. "I keep a journal called 'Meanderings,' and in it I write what I did today to make me feel happy. In another notebook, 'Reflections,' I write what other people tell me about myself that I need to listen to."

Remember the interconnected circles—a choice in one carries weight into all the others. A response to spiritual wholeness may also impact our work. A prominent musician reached a point where he abruptly stopped performing. He had lost the connection with his giftedness.

For three years, this musician and his wife literally secluded themselves far from the metropolitan madness, during which time he fished. He also rediscovered the Bible. He's now back on stage but with less recitals and more time for his family and fishing. A renewed faith now energizes his work with a different passion. As Bach said, "The aim and final reason of all music is the glory of God."

The Sailing Technique

Now that we've gone through the five interconnected circles, perhaps you are beginning to get a sense of just what might be out of balance within your life. Is there one circle which you've ignored? In considering your current work/job life, what can you add, alter, or amend to give you more control and happiness? Is there any way you can structure your work/job so as to add some of these important areas into it?

This latter question bears careful consideration. First, consider these following scenarios:

1. It's a beautiful, clear, blue and white Colorado winter day. The skiers are whisking down slopes of new powder. Two skiers slip into the lift-line and are carried upward for another run.

2. Night falls on a wave-battered Northern California coast. A man and a woman walk out to a rock outcropping overlooking the ocean as the sun sinks below the horizon.

3. Two volleyball teams spike, dive, and sweat on a sand court. Spectators, siding with neither team, applaud the effort as well as the results. The players are female/male, young/old, black/white, excited.

Do any of these scenarios sound like work? Dr. Tom Isgar, a management consultant from Colorado, planned it that way. And he got paid in the bargain. "We can make our work more like the not-work experiences we strive for. We can redesign some of our work so that it is fun."

And just what was Dr. Isgar doing?

In the first example, he was discussing career/life planning with a senior executive as well as the performance of several subordinates.

In the second, this scene was part of a four-hour drive down California's scenic coast highway during which time they conducted the initial program planning which led to a three-year organization improvement plan.

And in the last scene, the volleyball game was part of a team-building exercise within a large organization.

He depends on personal criteria to make work fun and healthier. "I like to play tennis so I design workshops with tennis time. I like fresh fruit so I ask that we have fruit and juice. Without exception I have experienced a positive response from clients. By acting on the items which make work more fun for me, I suggest ways in which others can make their own work fun. Most importantly, in doing so I improve the quality of my own working life while working with clients to improve the quality of theirs."

So Where Does It All Lead?

Only by considering our total self at the same time we seek either the "work" of our life or a "job" can we hope to be free to live. Sure, there will be times when we are tremendously out of balance, but the trick is to recognize just what circle has been given too much power or has been ignored.

"But wait," you might say. "There's just too much to consider. I can't get a handle on the big picture of my life."

You're absolutely right. That's why I have found it extremely beneficial to periodically put my "circles" down on paper and step back to get the entire effect. Amazing how things become focused when I suddenly realize where my attention has been centered. It also allows me to visualize the future and the overlapping impact of certain decisions on other parts of my life.

Now, I don't know about you, but I've never been good about writing inside circles. So for this visualization, I first attach five sheets of paper to a piece of freezer wrap. The important thing is that I see and think about my life as a whole; that it's laid out before me in one big picture.

Second, I consider just where I am *now* in my life. Let's face it, that's the coin of the realm, the only negotiable time frame I've got to work with. Sometimes we get so busy thinking ahead that the rest of our world in the here-and-now goes to "hell in a handbasket" before we're even aware of it.

After I look at the *now,* I can decide what immediate action steps need to be taken and what short-term goals need to be achieved. However, I also believe it is equally important to keep before you a vision of the future you prefer. I include such a future in my "now" picture so that I am constantly reminded just what direction I'm headed. (Later on, I also chart out a game plan with measurable goals and corresponding activities to work toward that future vision in incremental steps.)

Third, I don't always fill in all the spaces. Sometimes, it is enough just to become aware of interrelationships and places where I might want to alter course.

If you'll look at Figures 5.1 through 5.5 you'll notice

that each box urges me to think of the benefits as well as the penalties for continuing where I am going. Not infrequently, we set a so-called goal without really asking ourself just how we might benefit from an action. This must be balanced by also asking ourselves just what might be the penalty if we do not take action or if we do not achieve a specific goal.

Sometimes, the penalty is severe. For example, Elizabeth's penalty for not paying attention to her eczema when it first started was that it became progressively worse. And who knows, had she not re-balanced her life to spend more time with areas other than work, she might also have lost more than physical comfort.

You will also notice that each box has a section entitled "Impact on Other Areas." By thinking about and/or writing down what areas might be impacted, I have a clearer understanding as to accommodations which I might want to make in other areas. Or, I might also decide that the impact is too great and put some plans on hold. Lastly, I also like to leave room for "feelings." Let me explain this term a little more.

Although I'm an ex-debater by avocation and pride myself on making logical decisions, I have come to the realization that all of us ultimately respond to our lives with our feelings. On the surface I might claim that my decision is based solely on logic. However, the inner core reality could be that I'll feel guilty if I don't respond in a logical manner.

It might be that responding to feelings once got me in trouble, so, therefore, if I base my decision on logic, I feel that I'm safe. One woman told me that for most of her life she had always lived from the neck up, denying how she really felt because it meant making risky decisions. "Now I also listen to my heart."

With this in mind, I've learned to at least listen and record what I'm feeling as I think about each area. It tells me where I'm anxious, uptight, joyful, excited, maybe even scared. As you'll learn in Chapter Eight, some of these feelings could really be rooted in outdated or invalid attitudes. Getting such feelings into the open might be crucial to growth.

As I share this model with you, please keep in mind that each of us will respond to this model in different ways and fill in those areas which currently dominate the "now" of his/her life in a much different fashion.

Obviously, at this present moment, the Intellectual area (Figure 5.1) occupies the greatest chunk of both my time and energy. Since I am slowly beginning to meld work and job, I've divided this "boxed" circle into the areas that energize me, recognizing that within each area I will also find assignments which are "jobs." During this phase of my work, my writing has precluded most other activities save for some consulting assignments scheduled within a month from now when the bulk of this writing is over. Normally, there would be something in process under each one.

You'll notice that I have a category termed "exploration." This is for those intellectual pursuits which have nothing specifically to do with my "work" but are merely those things I wish to know more about.

For example, my husband and I are heading soon to Greece. I am not content to merely read tourist papers. I want to understand *more*. So my nightstand has books on Greek history, mythology, and literature. I am forever finding that there are things I would like to know about technology. Now, given the limited amount of time I have, this is something which truly takes a back seat. If I can hire it out, I'll wait to learn.

Figure 5.1   **Intellectual**

Activity	Activity Now	Benefits Of Doing Activity	Penalties of Not Doing Activity	Impact on Other Areas	Feelings
1. SPEAKING	• Multiple Dates	• Have it; Income	• Decrease Income	• Travel takes time	• Joy
2. WRITING	• Complete book due now	• Enjoy new experience • Feel relief when finished • Will have forum for speaking • Will (I hope) make a difference • Will make new contacts and friends	• Will lose 'face' to self • Will jeopardize reputation • Will have lost a valuable experience and opportunity	• Less time with family • Will need more exercise • Diminished cash flow while writing	• Joy • Apprehension • Excitement • Anticipation
3. CONSULTING	• Facilitate management retreat • New material	• Will refresh memory • Can add new material • Will enhance program • Will add to learning • Will be able to interact more effectively • Will become more comfortable with material	• Will be same with material • Might not perform as well • Lost credibility • Will have put associate in bad position	• No substantial impact on most • Added income • Cost of transparency • No other substantial impact • Will add income	• Some tedium • Some excitement • Eager • Curious
4. PROFESSIONAL DEVELOPMENT: Education, Membership, Meetings	• NSA	• Stay current • Maintain professional acquaintances • Networking • Possible work • Ability to share experiences	• Lose visibility among peers • Name not in directories	• Time commitment takes from all other areas	• Ambivalence • Friendship • Impatience
COMMUNITY DEVELOPMENT:	• None, too hard with traveling	• Help improve community quality of life • A world beyond war			• Concern • Guilt • Pride • Urgency
5. EXPLORATION Books, classes	• Read Greek material • Study voice	• Sense of historical perspective • New knowledge	• Boredom • Staying dormant • No expansion	• Cost of time and money • Reduce workload or family/friend time	• Curious • Envious • Delighted

Action Plan – Now: Priority: book, speaking engagements.
Activity – Near Future: Persuasion workshop, presentation for university faculty and management, creativity/goal-setting off-site retreat for client.
Activity – Near Future Desires: client development, begin attending meetings, develop support materials and lectures for book.
Preferred Future: Speaking engagements, newspaper column, a gathering place for intellectual sharing, Spanish fluency.

Since most areas are dormant until the book is completed, I considered the benefits of finishing this task and recorded my feelings when I thought about the benefits. Interestingly, when it came to penalties, I realized how much I felt that I would be unfaithful to myself if I did not complete this book. And I also had to acknowledge that while I wrote, "my reputation will be jeopardized if the book is not printed," this was just not the case. Instead, I would feel embarrassed and guilty, but my validity as a consultant would not be affected.

In looking at the impact of this work on other areas, it became clear that my family would need to be included in my effort. After all, I might not be able to come home on time, the housecleaning might be hit-and-miss, and my income would be lowered. Thanks to an understanding husband and the youngest at-home daughter, everyone has pitched in to compensate for this period of imbalance.

In considering the Material (Figure 5.2), I've divided this area into Haves, Needs, and Wants. The Haves are those significant material items which are already in my possession and require upkeep and/or money. The Needs are those things which are necessary items for the immediate future. For example, under "basics" I consider food, clothing, medical insurance, etc. You'll notice that I've also put current professional needs (brochure) in the same category. Ultimately, the money all comes from the same pot. Obviously, some needs are also more pressing than others.

Under Wants, I place those material items which are future desires of a more distant nature. However, were my car to die on me tomorrow, getting a new or used car would become a more critical need rather than a passive want.

I consider all of these items, and I do mean ALL, as discretionary. I have a certain standard in mind when I think

Figure 5.2   **Material**

Category	Item	Benefits	Penalties	Impact On Other Areas	Feelings
1. HAVES IMMEDIATE	• Rental home • Our home	• Location, price, responsibility	• Overhead increases • Gardening chores • Different recreation • In California a must	• Tax implications • Freedom of movement • No room for other acquisitions	• Comfortable • Wistful • Free
	• Automobile • Computer	• It runs, interior fine • Time, energy productivity	• Disaster	• Critical to work	• So so • Grateful
	• Office	• Less distraction, productivity, organization			• Grateful • More sane
2. NEEDS THROUGH OUT YEAR	• Basics • College tuition • Vacation summer/winter • New Brochure	• Obvious	• Kids work, loans, scholarship	• Marriage/work	
3. WANTS	• Ranch property and house	• Achieve mutual dream—serenity	• Won't be able to give Bill his wish	• Marriage/work • Might mean giving up vacation	
	• New car	• Mileage, investment, appearance			• Joy • Pleasure • Sense of "arrival"
	• Upgraded computer • Adventurous travel for extended time	• Increased output, investment • Knowledge, experiences to write and speak about			

Action Plan: Haves—monetary requirement. Wants—Monetary requirement.
Preferred Future: Savings plan for retirement.

of everything from clothes to food to vacations. By judging the benefits and penalties of attaining that standard, I can make more appropriate decisions ranging from "no go" to "raise/lower" the standard. The point is that I remain in control. Actually, I should rephrase that as "we" remain in control. Material standards are a compromise between marriage partners.

Interestingly enough, even though I did not completely fill in this section, I realized that I actually had tremendous flexibility when it came to material decisions. That revelation in and of itself produced a very freeing effect. Additionally, just by thinking about the benefits and penalties of some possessions, it

Figure 5.3

Emotional

People Now	How to Touch	Benefits	Penalties	Impact on Other Areas	Feelings
1. BILL	• Time spent with, calls	• Time to share • Time to be	• Lose precious time • Grow apart	• Could take class together • Work in good shape now	• Warm • Supported
2. CHILDREN/ GRANDCHILDREN Heather Holly, Phil, Todd	• Time spent with, calls • Calls, letters, visits	• May become friends			
3. MY FAMILY Mother Susan John, Jeanne	• Sept, vacation, calls, letters • Calls, letters, visits • Calls, letters, go see?				
4. FRIENDS Lola, Barb, John	• Calls, get-togethers				
5. FRIENDS TO TOUCH Lea, Bev, Sue	• Letters, calls, visits				
6. SELF	• Moments • Meanderings • Manicures				

Action Plan: Where is greatest need? Who first, second, etc., and how??
Preferred Future: One full day for family, one full day for Bill, one full day for friends every two weeks.

became clear that buying a home at this time is a comfortable decision and that my preferred future (represented here by "wants") is still on target.

In the Emotional "boxed" circle (Figure 5.3), I include not only my immediate family, but also friends whom I currently have as well as new friends whom I would like to know better. There is nothing significant about the order in which people are listed. Nor, for the sake of this illustration, did I list all the people.

By writing down the various ways I might touch all these people, I become aware of just whom I have neglected. I am also prompted to consider where might be the greatest mutually beneficial touchstone or where I might be most needed.

And I've found it

Figure 5.4

Physical

Category	Activity Now	Benefit	Penalty	Impact	Feelings
1. EXERCISE	• Class at least 5x/week • Run 3 miles at least once a week	• Productivity • Sleep better • More energy	• Lose muscle tone	• Book has been my excuse • Dinner is delayed • Must often choose between meetings or exercise	• Guilty • Frustrated
2. NUTRITION	• Too much meat • Too much 'partying' last few months				• Concerned but getting better
3. SLEEP	• Average 7 hours	• Alert	• Irritable • Dull	• Can't read late at night	• Satisfied about sleep • Envious of others who can get more out of a day
4. CHORES	• Housework				
6. HEALTH (OVERALL)	• Good health				

Action Plan – Must exercise more faithfully; go on fruit/salad diet; increase water intake.

very important to add myself. Sometimes, it is easy to become so wrapped up in touching others that we forget about making time for ourselves. I am slowly learning that time spent on myself is a way of re-connecting with me. This might be something as simple as getting a manicure, splurging on café au lait and croissants when I probably should be doing something more constructive, or taking a weekend away by myself for a personal retreat.

It's not easy, I admit. The cultural programming, particularly if you are married, still insists that togetherness is a daily mandate; that "mothering" must take precedence over self. But I think I'm a better spouse, companion, and mother when I'm refreshed by such times.

In the Physical area (Figures 5.4) you'll notice that I place "sleep" and "chores" in this category. If I look at this and realize that I've been getting about five hours' sleep for an extended length of time, I know my body is headed for trouble.

Figure 5.5

Spiritual

Category	Activity Now	Benefit	Penalty	Impact	Feelings
1. MEDITATION	• Daily—meditation music	• Centering • Calm • Direction	• Haste • Worry	• Takes time from sleep	• Lost without it
2. FORMAL MEANS	• Sunday service • Retreats	• Time out		• No substantial impact	
3. LEISURE	• Ocean walks (on hold)				
4. READINGS	• On hold				

Action Plan – Ocean walks, reading must begin.
Preferred Future – Deeper spiritual development.

Under "chores," keeping a clean house has always been a top priority for me—and one that sometimes has caused me difficulty. In fact to be honest, I make Mr. Clean look like a fake. But I'm learning. I've discovered that one can become just as out of balance insisting that everything sparkle simultaneously. On the flip side, I've also ascertained that sometimes a day spent washing windows and cleaning closets can recharge my batteries as much as a night on the town can for someone else. I just FEEL better when it's done.

Lastly, under Spiritual (Figure 5.5), I write those in-process items. Although meditation is a daily event for me, it is sometimes hard to wake up an extra hour earlier. When I wrote this particular chart, I reminded myself of its benefits. I also realized that while ocean walks and readings are favorites, my current work has also curtailed these activities. I resolved to walk this weekend!

Unless you're a compulsive person who just loves charts and graphs, I wouldn't go crazy over this model and spend days filling in the blanks. I've found that sometimes it is enough to see the basics and merely think about the implications in other areas. Note the word "see." It is important that this chart be placed somewhere and studied anytime it is used.

Then again, at times of confusion, I've found it helpful to use a written system as a means of channeling my thoughts and making some action steps for future goals—but all based upon where I am now. So, depending upon the area where there is confusion, I'll fill in as many spaces as needed and again post the results.

Please do not be intimidated by my system. I merely offer it to you as a sample which can be adapted for your personal use. Remember, everything is flexible—even if it is in writing. As we grow, everything changes: from people to preferred futures.

I would suggest that maybe, just once in a while, giving yourself this exercise can be a good way of experimenting with sailing without actually climbing into the boat; of letting yourself "try on" possible decisions; of getting a clearer handle on what is *really* important in your life.

Another way to get a bearing on how you are navigating in your sailboat is to conduct a year-end or mid-year check. The following questions stimulate much awareness as to the "now" of our lives. I keep a journal and answer these questions twice a year. It also then helps me to realize just where I am spending my time and what are my priorities. I also have a simple monthly log in which I take the five areas of my life and collect just what happened in those areas. It has a wonderful way of allowing me to realize that time does not just pass me by. Often, I am amazed at how much I am in control and how balanced I actually am!

Reflective questions (for year-end or mid-year check)

1. What were your top priorities in time, money and energy?
2. What were your finest accomplishments?
3. What were your biggest surprises?
4. What were your biggest disappointments?
5. What were your most significant decisions?
6. What people were you closest to?
7. What stressed you the most?
8. Where did you travel for fun?
9. What lessons have you learned
10. Who or what were you most angry at?
11. What did you procrastinate on?
12. Summarize the year (or six-month period) in a word.

The answers to these questions allow me to step back and see just where my time has gone. I can also analyze some answers by placing them in A through C categories:

"A" tasks are:	*"B" tasks* are:	*"C" tasks* are:
urgent	self-initiated	started by others
now	important long-term	now
highly valuable	often hard	easy
critical	time-consuming	fast
hard to negotiate	complex	simple to do

"It's not enough to be busy. So are the ants. What are you busy about?"
— *Thoreau*

Summary

1. Working and quality living can go together—
   just as wind goes with a sailboat.
2. Balance is interconnectedness, the connection of
   all five parts of our human existence: intellectual
   stimulus (work/job), material possession
   (money and "things"), emotional stability
   (love), physical well-being, and spiritual
   wholeness. If one circle is not connected, or if
   one overshadows the others for an extended
   length of time, imbalance results.
3. Balance also implies knowing when we are out
   of balance and which areas of our life have been
   neglected.
4. Balance is not a static condition. Like a sailboat
   that requires constant handling, we need to
   constantly monitor and sometimes accept
   imbalance until we are ready to change course.
5. The most important part is learning how to stay
   connected; learning how to sail.
6. Our intellectual stimulus is defined as that which
   claims our concentration, utilizes our talents and
   preferred skills, and results in something in
   which we can claim "I did it." The goal is to find
   the "work" of our lives, that activity which uses
   our giftedness.
7. Money can buy us things we need and want. It is
   also an external symbol of what someone else
   thinks of our work. Our wants and attitudes
   about money, however, can keep us in bondage.
   The key to staying in balance seems to be in
   knowing why you are making the material

choice, what impact it will have on the other areas, and then maintaining balance (or regaining balance) after that choice.

8. Choices for the "work" of our lives might alter our material possessions.

9. Love is critical to human existence. It influences longevity and contentment. Work and lifestyle decisions can positively or negatively impact love. The characteristics that make someone good at "work" are the opposite of those needed to be good at "love." We really do wear many hats, and we must know when to put each one on.

10. It is equally important to balance exercise, nutrition and recreation into the plan of our lives.

11. An understanding of balance is essential in making life-giving, free-to-live, work decisions.

Chapter Six

Eeney, Meeney, Miney, Mo

We are but the instruments of heaven; our work is not design but destiny.
— *Bulwer-Lytton, English poet*

I doubt anyone would ever accuse my husband of being a clothes horse. When we first met, his wardrobe was tasteful but sparse. In short order, my love of bargains and gift-giving soon began to fill his closet. "Look," he said one morning in frustration, "I love you, but please don't buy me any more shirts. How I hate to get up and make a decision!"

I hadn't thought about it that way. The opportunity to choose *can* be too much.

Although I like Bulwer-Lytton's quote because it capsulizes my idea of "giftedness," I nevertheless wish heaven could be more specific. Sometimes it doesn't seem fair that Biblical Samuel got a call in the middle of the night and bingo! His career was signed, sealed and delivered. For many of us, locating the work of our lives is a trial-and-error process. There are just so many choices.

And so we unwrap our giftedness slowly, unfolding tissue, peering between each layer, waiting to catch our breath before we see the actual gift. Some move on and find other gifts to open. It's not unusual.

A recent article published in *The Executive Female* reported that ten successful professionals (male and female) all responded "no" when asked, "Is what you are doing now what you originally had expected to be doing?" Some career counselors estimate that as many as seven major switches occur in a lifetime.

For others, giftedness is a present which can be immediately unwrapped and used with enthusiasm. It comes from a Greek word, "Enthousiasmos," meaning "possessed by a god within." (See heaven did have a say-so after all.) We can indeed be possessed—enthused—by our work.

Sandy, a single parent raising three teenagers, has taught elementary school for over twenty years. Ask her about her work and her face glows. "Why, I love it. It's my life." She's bewildered that I even had to ask! Lyricist Sammy Kahn once told an audience that "if they saw how much fun I have writing songs, I think they wouldn't pay me." From the time my gynecologist followed his grandfather around on house calls, he knew he wanted to be a doctor. Hundreds of babies later, my doctor friend can still say eagerly, "I love it! Women are wonderful!"

Lest you think this "possessed" group has it easy in the decision-making department, don't forget that they, too, are also responsible for maintaining balance by the choices made in other life areas.

So What Now?

Hopefully by now you're beginning to become aware of what might be the causes for your pit or where an imbalance might be present, what immediate actions might be required to gain some control of either work or a balance in living, and what impact your picture of "living" has on a work choice. More decisions are in the offing.

This chapter provides an overview for making decisions within two settings: the corporate (where you work for someone) and the entrepreneurial (where you work for yourself). We'll also look at some examples of "unfolding" so that you might observe the trial-and-error process.

If experience is the best teacher, then I've assembled some good tutors for you. Pay attention to how they explored, what choices were made for balance, what imbalance might still remain. Most of all, consider this your support team. You're not alone.

But first, let's add two more possibilities into the cerebral processor—to prepare you for this unfolding.

More In The Exploration Process

Creativity

In the last chapter, how did you feel when you read about Dr. Isgar's ability to add personal pleasure to his work routine? Did you wish that you could put some fun into your current or prospective work? Did you notice that he structured work activities to include recreation and nutrition? These are parts of the physical area which often become ignored with rapid-paced work. Or perhaps you might have thought, "Oh, that's easy for him. He's a consultant."

May I suggest that what allowed Isgar to even consider such additions was not his actual profession. Burned-out, stressed-out, in-the-pits consultants exist everywhere. No, the consulting practice was not the root for such work decisions. It was his ability to think creatively.

The creative person sees beyond the obvious, finds connections, thinks in terms of possibilities rather than impossibilities. The person who can channel a right-brain activity says "why not!" instead of "cannot!".

Consider these creative choices: A psychologist takes his clients mountain climbing. He loves the outdoors and they learn to trust, communicate, and risk. A sales executive is an amateur photographer. With permission from her clients, she takes candid as well as artistic shots within client companies. She sends them the photos as gifts *and* she makes a lot of sales. Jane needs exercise, but the class times at the local recreation center conflict with work and family. She talks to the Personnel Department and gets approval to lead an aerobics class twice a week at lunch time for interested colleagues.

Can you see the integration of other life areas? All connections. All creative wanderings that put many pieces of quality life into a work setting.

Think creatively about potential new work. Think connections. Colonel Sanders decided that other people would enjoy his mom's fried chicken. A wine press at a harvest festival became Gutenberg's inspiration for the printing press. An ex-surfer runs a windsurfing school in Hawaii.

But creativity also requires a willingness to depart from the normal course of action and remain courageous in the face of criticism, skepticism, and doubting Thomases. You can recognize the doubters by the words they use.

Killer phrases are everywhere:
- That's stupid.
- It will never work.
- We don't have the time.
- We tried it before.
- It'll cost too much money.

Care to add some killer phrases which you've heard recently? This exercise will alert you to the words others use to point out shortcomings rather than benefits; why some things won't work rather than how to make things better. Come on, think of two:

    1. _____
    2. _____

Just as there are trigger-happy doubters on the outside, there is a real sharpshooter on the inside. More frequently than not, an idea is squashed by mental thumbs down inside of us. When you begin to think beyond the obvious, particularly about choices that will change your "work" or life, have you said this to yourself:
- People will think I'm crazy.
- Who do I think I am to try that!
- My wife (husband) will kill me.
- My parents (lover, mentor, whoever) will be terribly disappointed in me.
- As soon as I bring up my idea, someone will kick it apart.
- What if it doesn't work!?

Now it's your turn. Care to venture any killer phrases which you use to halt further consideration of a new or different direction? Go ahead, try for two:

    1. _____
    2. _____

If you can recognize killer phrases, perhaps you can

halt the guerrilla warfare which prevents you from at least exploring creative choices.

The Road Not Taken

Two concepts rest in this phrase. We owe the first to Robert Frost, the crusty New England poet who penned that taking the road less traveled had "made all the difference." Breaking with tradition, following a creative path, going against the tide, doing the unexpected are all less-traveled roads—roads not ordinarily taken by the majority. It might be that your choices entail leaving the well-worn career path or lifestyle and striking out in a new direction.

The second concept cares nothing about how many people travel down a road. Rather, it invites you to re-examine a path not taken in the past and to consider walking down it now! This concept is seldom discussed and yet holds tremendous potential in understanding the movement of our lives and in making choices. I first heard this phrase in connection with Progoff's work. In fact, "the road not taken" titles one section of the Intensive Journal. But whether or not one ever participates in the Intensive Journal workshops, the "road not taken" concept is critical.

The movement of your life, up to this very minute, has been marked by decisions, some made by you, some made by others, and some made sheerly by circumstance. These decisions sent you down certain paths—paths which led to where you are today. However, this does not mean that you cannot go back and explore the road you didn't take! The conditions which created the road taken long ago might indeed have altered or even vanished.

For example, in looking back over stages of my life, I suddenly remembered that my father had wanted me to take singing lessons and I had refused. Painfully shy, I *died* at piano recitals. The thought of having to perform in another one was too much. But I feel different now about myself.

To walk down that "road not taken," I took a singing lesson. I took lots of them. Great fun. Now—where possible, I incorporate music in my programs.

At face value this might seem like a rather mundane road to explore. But I have always felt a twinge of envy at Broadway stars and cabaret singers. No more. No so-called vain regrets. Dealing with that buried memory was as important as if I had discovered a new talent and direction.

What a win-win proposition! Here's one other consideration in the "road not taken" concept: nothing is forever. Just because I decided that at this time in my life singing is not a profession for me, there's wonderful freedom in knowing that I can go back at any time and once again, try journeying down that road.

The Corporate Career—
Moving Around Inside

Any Which Way You Want
One of the more common and dangerous errors in seeking the "work" of your life or giftedness is to think that there are only two alternatives when you work for someone else: out or up. The "out" choice to another organization might still not tap your skills if they remain unidentified or if you're holding onto damaging attitudes. "Out" to entrepreneurship might mean longer hours, less freedom, greater financial risk. As for "up," long considered the only legitimate way to success, hear this: it's not the only way.

Let's try that again: *up is not the only way.* And who would know this better than Dr. Beverly Kaye, author of a book by the very title and a nationally recognized corporate career management consultant. For over three decades, Dr. Kaye has worked with hundreds of corporations across the United States to help employees discover their preferred skills and point those talents in the direction indicated by the individual's entire "life" picture. That direction might be any which way but up!

"Society does people a real injustice by telling them that the vertical, traditional move is the only way. After all, just how many people can fit on the point of a pyramid? We can't all move up—but we can all grow. There should always be a challenge in your career, something that requires your all. But it doesn't have to come from the next rung on the ladder above you."

In addition to the standard vertical move into a higher salary and title, Dr. Kaye lists five other directions to consider: moving across (lateral), growing in place (enrichment), looking around (exploratory), moving down (realignment) and lastly, moving out (relocation).

The Lateral Move

"A sideways move more often makes more sense than people realize," says Kaye. "It allows you to develop new skills, broaden your base of knowledge, change geographical locations and/or colleagues, and maybe even reach a faster growth area of the company. For example, a loan office might move to another branch. He's still a loan officer, but the branch, customers, and employees are different."

In other cases, a lateral move can take existing skills and transfer them into a different position but with equivalent pay and status. Debbie G. (fictitious name) was a marketing officer who gambled on a possible decrease in pay to transfer to the personnel relations office so that she might work more with people. Not only did she maintain her present salary, but her newfound enthusiasm for the personally rewarding position led to a dramatic rise in salary and grade level in less than a year.

Kaye insists, "Sudden benefits are not surprising when people are doing what they really like and do well. Organizations only benefit when their employees are in the 'like' and 'do-well' jobs."

The Enrichment Move

Instead of moving across, enhancing the current position could be a strong option. You already observed a number of cases where individuals added portions of other life areas to their "work." Kaye believes that there are also ways to make a current job more exciting, more challenging. "But the individual has to devise these; the company isn't going to do it for him or her," she says.

Karen W., a communications specialist for an international manufacturer of computer products, decided that just writing the company newsletter was not enough challenge. "I accepted responsibility for the corporate identity package which would give me a lot of visibility within the company. I also volunteered to take on a brochure for the personnel department. Now, my paycheck is almost like a bonus. I truly enjoy what I'm doing."

As we noted earlier, the enrichment of your job might mean adding things other than what might normally be entitled as "work." A priest in an inner-city parish began to experience the pangs of burnout. So much to do, so little to do it with, so hard to reach the people who needed help. To correct that imbalance, he began getting back into a pastime long since neglected—music. Weekend jam sessions with some of the neighbors attracted a crowd. Within short order, he bartered an old piano from a local bar, placed it in the parish hall and began offering piano lessons to children in the area. By enhancing his current position with the use of another talent, his flock is increasing and so is his level of satisfaction.

The Exploration Move

In the exploration option, an employee researches new opportunities to use already uncovered talents as well as to discover hidden or dormant skills. With Dr. Kaye's help, an unhappy computer draftsman finally realized that his skills were totally people-oriented. A move to the planning department dramatically changed the work field, and yet his satisfaction was still not hitting number ten on the charts. Another workshop refined those "people skills" as "teaching skills." He then opted to put on mini-seminars introducing new employees to the department. In this case, both the exploration and enrichment option made sense.

The Realignment Move

Ever so slowly, our changing value system is making it more feasible to look at downscaling as a way for gaining control and balance within one's life. Although the move is still difficult because it's the exact opposite of the cultural programming, "downshifting" is catching hold.

"It's hard for the failure stigma not to be attached to a downward move," relates Dr. Kaye. "But both employers and individuals can benefit from taking a healthier view of this move. A higher position does not always bring the anticipated personal rewards. There are those who find out after a promotion to a managerial slot that they really don't like it at all. They don't like the pressure, the time demands, the intrusions on their personal life."

The former president of a large publishing company explained his choice for a downward move in these terms. "My ego wasn't satisfied by titles. While I was president, the company became more successful. We rose from $8 million to $40 million. And I hated it. I became all consumed by the bottom line. At my request, I moved into a division with ten people."

Another composite example:

A medical researcher, noted for his brilliance in new product development, made the inevitable move through the ranks until reaching a position where he managed an entire research division working on cardiovascular instrumentation. A different type of paperwork poured across his desk. Employee performance needed to be monitored. Orders had to be given, work teams harmonized, and salary reviews made. A classic pit was in the making: stress, fatigue, irritability, strained family relationships, and much imbalance.

Let the truth be known: he wanted to be a researcher, not a manager. Thankfully, he realigned himself back into the old spot. To his astonishment, his wife broke open the champagne. The researcher had felt that she wanted him to make the top slot when in reality, she secretly wanted him back where he was happy but was afraid he didn't want to move down.

The Relocation Move

If the company had not been progressive enough to restructure job categories to accommodate people like the medical researcher, his move might have been out.

Such was the case of a director of engineering in a large computer firm. He loved tinkering with the product as a hands-on designer. His interpersonal skills were strong one-on-one, but as a manager he swam like a landed salmon. His outward move put him back in the water as vice president of a small computer company, where he is integrally involved in the design and marketing of the product.

Dr. Kaye admits it's not easy convincing a company that a move out of the corporation has as much validity as the other options. "They worry that they'll lose their best, most valuable employees. But if a person is unhappy, the organization isn't going to get a full effort from him/her anyway. And sometimes, the only position a person can take is a path out of the company."

Mike B., now senior industrial relations executive for a consulting firm.

When we first met Mike, he had determined that his first responsibility for getting out of the "people" pit was to rearrange his reaction to the vice president's autocratic style and temper tantrums.

As a newcomer in the area, he began a concerted effort to attend whatever evening meetings he could find within his profession, started to network on weekends, and also explored lateral moves within the corporation.

The corporate search turned up a dismal picture. It appeared that autocracy plus a rigid caste system dominated the corporate culture. Long-time employees, plus a friend in the personnel department, warned him not to "make waves." "Just accept the good salary and keep your mouth shut."

For a talented person with strong ambition, that

option was tasteless. Instead, he determined to remain until such time as a highly attractive growth opportunity presented itself. In the meantime, he accepted assignments which others didn't want and kept the corporate game in play.

"When I finally resigned to accept a challenging position that had been offered through networking, my work spoke for itself. I left well, despite the conflicts with my vice president."

⚜

Whether the move is up, down, around, across, or out, we do have choices and the responsibility to ASK for what we want. Granted, we might have to seek outside assistance in determining just what we *really* want to ask for and the reality of that request. (The self-administered Career Leverage Inventory developed by Kaye is just one example of many available external resources used by career counselors.)

In whatever fashion, by whatever means you move toward a decision, the point remains: "There are multiple ways, endless paths to follow. It makes very little sense in today's business world to limit yourself to an upward path," Kaye concludes.

The Corporate Career— Moving in From The Outside

The Financial Move

George G. returned to his uncle's corporation because his public-relations practice fell short of its mark. Sandy R. opted for a sales position with a manufacturing company when the income from teaching proved too miniscule for a single homeowner. Ronda S., a speech therapist, felt the same financial crunch as well as a host of other imbalances.

Although financial need pressed each into working for somebody else, their levels of happiness and growth have varied because of other choices, including the way each chose to see himself or herself.

George G., retired senior executive, multinational corporation.

Ten years earlier, George had left his uncle's company as a vice president, doubting his ability and success. Now, he returned from a failed venture at a much lower position. And it was there, in retrospect, where he should have stayed. "The happiest years of my life: I wasn't a manager."

But society (and George's own personal sense of success) did not acknowledge achievement as anything but upward mobility and increased income. Wherever the company pushed him, up he went. Making any other choice was too frightening.

"I think choices represent a scary idea. I expect I'm almost the type of person who requires structure, who should have stayed in the Armed Forces for thirty years. I don't really want to be this way. But it's scary to think about doing something else."

Because George didn't choose something else, his retirement now feels tight, distressed, empty. In the first chapter, he candidly shared how fear of failure was keeping him from fully exploring his artistic abilities. A narrow focus in past choices seems to have also created an even narrower retirement. When one's nose remains plastered to the grindstone, other areas and interests aren't even glimpsed peripherally.

❧

I truly celebrate George's ability to verbalize for others what he is just now beginning to discover for himself. His candor helps all of us. And by honestly looking at what has been, he can—if he chooses—begin to regain the balance in the neglected areas of his life.

For Sandy R., the move from elementary education into selling industrial couplings, has precipitated balance in some areas and imbalance in others. "Sailing" is difficult at times.

❧

Sandy R., traveling sales representative.

Before leaving the teaching profession permanently, Sandy had taken a year's sabbatical to develop a teaching module for the U.S. Senate Computer Center. Although offered a management position, she returned to teaching because she missed her friends and the children.

The need for a more substantial income became a great concern. The second—the need for love. "In teaching, I was substituting a relationship with the kids for a relationship with a man. I was giving it all away because I wasn't emotionally tied to anyone." She turned to an employment counselor as a way to find an alternative to teaching.

Besides income, the "job" has brought some internal problems. "I think teaching was a shelter. When I was a teacher, I doubted my ability to do anything else. Teaching was a way to quickly lose self-confidence with adults and the ability to work with peers. When the employment counselor found this job, I was intrigued but scared. Now I know I can drive up to an oil refinery. I can read mechanical drawings. I know I'm responsible for the accounts I bring in.

"If I ever get in a position where I want to leave, I can go off and search for adventure. At least now I have a choice. Although this job is hard, teaching was harder on the emotions. My sales manager had first said that he would never hire a woman. But we worked and grew together, which resulted in my being above quota every quarter."

But there are imbalances along the way. Her perfectionism as a teacher has translated into long hours, lots of travel. "I feel like there's not enough of me to go around. Sometimes I unplug my phone and read a book. Now, I've got this unknown virus which has lasted for months: headaches, constant exhaustion, and a low-grade fever. But I don't think it's job related."

When asked about teaching, Sandy's eyes begin to brim with tears, much to her surprise. "I will never do anything that will give me the sense of satisfaction that I had with teaching. What an impact: you can make or break a child; either destroy or build their self-confidence. I didn't realize [in reference to her tears] how much I had invested with them. I miss them."

⁂

Amazing, isn't it, what we can learn about ourselves through choices. For all the apparent dilemma of balance which Sandy is beginning to realize, her outlook allows her to be flexible with herself and, therefore, to alter course.

"Change is growth. Anytime you move into the unknown you grow. The more self-knowledge, the more you have to give. Allowing yourself the opportunity to grow in business and personally is the only way you can say, 'This is who I am,'" adds Sandy.

During the year's exploration which preceded her entry into an educational equipment company, Ronda S. carefully considered all of the areas which were out of balance and just how a work setting would need to be structured in order to challenge and excite her.

⚜

Ronda S., sales representative.

"As a speech therapist, I was always working on someone who needed to be 'fixed.' I wondered what it would be like to be creative and cause a change in other people's lives. I knew I liked to be with people in a creative rather than regimented setting. I needed to be in charge, make decisions. I also like the idea of bringing together friends from different environments, putting together different pieces of information, being a central networker."

When she sold her house and moved to another city to be with her boyfriend, financial and emotional stability increased. She knew that whatever work she found, there would have to be time allowed for him, enough income to support her needs, and time for exercise and church attendance.

"What I found is a blend of education with technology. I can set my own time and I move to people rather than them coming to me. My clients are all school districts. I not only understand but can have sympathy for their paperwork, as well as financial burdens. And I am finding lots of ways to be

creative with new applications for the equipment
every day. I am also able to put people together so
they can collaborate on the use of the equipment and
learn from each other. As for balance, I am still
missing the ingredient of really 'making a difference' so I might make it up with some volunteer
work. I don't want material things to take precedence."

The Balance Move

When we think of someone "closing up shop" to
return to work for someone else, the more common
response is to think, "Well, they just couldn't make enough
money at it." Pretty fair assumption. But there *are* other
reasons behind such a decision.

*Paul O. (fictitious name), former real estate
sales executive, now escrow agent.*

For five years, Paul had worked hard building up
a real estate business in San Francisco. He spent
weekends taking clients around, met with other
agents during the evenings, and always found his
telephone answering machine filled with calls
whenever he went away. Financially, life was fine.
But he wasn't.

"It was crazy. I never had enough time for me.
Or for that matter, even enough time to develop a
significant relationship."

When he was thirty-six, Paul stopped making
deals. He accepted a nine-to-five job with an hourly
salary at a small escrow company. "I got my life
back. I moved into a tiny apartment, which simpli-
fied everything from cleaning to the quantity of

furniture. I began taking evening classes just for the heck of it. I read books. I took up camping. I basically started to enjoy my life."

As for money, Paul made an interesting discovery. "I had always worried about money. You know, having enough to get what I wanted, make payments and all that jazz. As soon as I decided to *stop* worrying about money, I have always had enough!! Not an overabundance, mind you, but always enough. That's sure better than worrying!"

The Sit-Tight Move

Although at first glance, this might sound like a contradiction, another choice for work/balance/living might be to stay exactly where you are (provided you are happy), while at the same time making plans for a new growth pattern. It might be that the time is coming when a "road not taken" will become the chosen path. Retirement might be in the offing or a dormant interest might flower. Whatever the reason, I believe it is not only healthy but vital that we maintain growth in numerous areas of interest.

Case in point: Few would deny the fact that Charles is a very good lawyer. The law firm considers him an asset and there's a good working relationship with his colleagues. But Charles has a passion: writing music. Now that he no longer has to "prove" himself and take tricky cases, there's time for his music. He has started taking classes in music writing, attending seminars, and playing the piano more frequently. His goal at some time: leave the firm and do nothing but write music.

Daryl P., (fictitious name) director of public works for one of the fastest-growing metropolitan cities in the nation.

Daryl has a grip like a bear and a hand just about as big. The massive deer's head hanging on his office wall attests to the fact that he is every bit the hunter he claims to be.

"It's my avocation. I love hunting and fishing. In fact, that's how I became a civil engineer. I had a summer job surveying in the mountains and discovered that I could end a day's work and head to the woods."

He's also uncovered a gift for patience and humor. Handling any city job with its attendant political turmoil, the rush of steady development, and a staff of 160, demands the same skill as waiting in a duck blind. "Some things you just have to wait out," he chuckles, "and if you relax, stay calm, the problems often resolve themselves."

Throughout his decade-plus career with the city, Daryl has also made sure that he creates balance for both the avocation as well as his family. "Instead of taking the first raise I was offered, I asked for more time off. Now I've got plenty built up and can head up to our ranch retreat or just off to nearby game preserves. Sometimes alone, sometimes with family, sometimes with my friends."

Life is fine. But Daryl has a dream. "I'd like to make this even more pleasurable. When the kids are gone, we're thinking about spending six months here and maybe six months at the ranch. I'd like to do consulting in advocacy or planning. But when we head to the ranch, maybe I can put together hunting trips for a fee. Right now, my wife and I are just exploring."

⚜

Driving up the freeway one evening during this past Christmas season, I was startled to see a long row of Christmas lights floating at what seemed to be sixty feet in mid-air. "What the heck," I muttered squinting through the dusty windshield. Finally, I approached the lights glowing at the end of an empty tract of land. Now illuminated by street lamps, I realized that the colored lights were not performing some trick in levitation. They were strung along the boom of a gigantic construction crane crouched beside the foundation of a new high-rise. Even in the midst of ordinary, daily labor, someone had decided that the piece of machinery should participate in the holiday celebration!

Can we humans expect less from our daily labor? Making choices for moving around a company, or into one, or—as we'll read in a minute—out of one and into our own, is part of our need to celebrate. We don't want to feel left out of any of the joy which might be ours to claim. But nobody can do it for us. Maybe that's why there were also plenty of other construction cranes with dark colorless booms sitting in solemn silence throughout that holiday season. I think they were waiting.

The Entrepreneurial Choice

"Get out on a limb. That's where the fruit is." I have no idea what Will Rogers had in mind when he made this statement, but it certainly applies to the mind-set of an entrepreneur, the self-employed individual. Of course, there are as many different kinds of "fruit" as there are "limbs."

Probably the number one golden apple is independence, the ability to answer to no one but yourself. This can be a large misconception. Depending upon the nature of your work, Uncle Sam, labor unions, EEO boards and public agencies dictate much of your life. When you are the "boss" (even if you boss only yourself), the work can be both your master and mistress, your slave driver and lover. It *all depends* upon your choices for balance as to who does most of the driving.

For this reason, I think the healthiest way to look at the "independence" fruit is that it first feeds your giftedness and quality of life. Note that I did not say independence "increases your income, lets you take vacations more often and means you don't have to deal with irritating people and egos."

The reality is that despite the enormous starts in new businesses, the majority will fail within the first two years. The reality is that it could well take two or three years before you might be able to even live off your income much less make a profit. The reality is that whether you offer a service or product, people become your primary concern. If you don't deal with the customer or client directly, you'll still have to effectively manage the other people who will.

This doesn't mean don't follow your dream. But it does mean make your choices wisely. As long as you focus on using your talents and interests, you're off to a good start. A false start is getting into something different "just because." There are plenty of good books, courses, and consultants who will tell you the prerequisites for an enterprise: prior experience or the willingness to go through training, an analysis of the marketplace and competitors, management skills, accurate financial assessment and budgeting, and a well-conceived marketing plan.

But in this book, my concern is that you consider why you make the choice, what impact it will have on the quality of your life, and how you structure that "work" along with other equally important decisions in life.

For example, an entrepreneurial decision might come from lifestyle considerations. A financial analyst from Los Angeles opened a ski shop in the mountains of Vermont and gained back the family he had ignored. By the same token, the company president who refused to adjust lifestyle requirements and take less than her $6,000 per month salary out of her business ended up losing it.

Ah, the interconnectedness of choices!

Consider this balance: While waiting for the arrival of her third baby, a housewife who loved to sew accessories for the baby's room discovered a need for her giftedness. Now, seven children later and with a portfolio of everything from wall hangings to baby crib bumpers, she has a multi-million-dollar manufacturing company. She's discovered other talents and is ready to spread her wings in new directions, with the same husband of long ago. By the same token, a colleague recently told me about a woman who owns a quite unique gift store but runs herself and the family ragged. "She's great at what she does; she's shattered by how she does it."

Ah, balance.

Or an entrepreneurial decision might rest in the ability to continue the same line of work but at a different pace and setting. Sean F., the once-burned-out cameraman for ABC and former photographer for the California Angels, has now created a new line of work with challenge and excitement: video productions concerning nature. "We've filmed bass fishing tournaments, snowmobiling and ice fishing, and completed a feature on river steelhead. As of today, our Outdoor News Network show is scheduled to be broadcast over the Satellite Programming Network (SPN) within the next few months. We climb mountains now to get pictures. And we like to incorporate the human spirit within the beauty of the natural surroundings. I can pick projects and be discriminating because our overhead is very slim."

On the flip side of the coin, a former *Los Angeles Times* still photographer who captured history-making photos of presidents, astronauts, and even wayward animals now has a video production corporation and studio for filming corporate programming documentaries, and commercials. His state-of-the-art facility requires a different pace and harmony. "Our projects use a multitude of ideas, from a multitude of people, with sophisticated hardware, all of which is filtered into a complete production on site."

Both entrepreneurs, similar choices, different balances in work setting. Vive le difference.

There is one advance warning. If entrepreneurial adventure occurs as a mid-life career switch, be prepared to make alterations in the way you sail through life. According to *Fortune* magazine, "The second-careerist's biggest problem might seem to be maintaining his or her accustomed standard of living. Incomes tend to be low, often no more than one-third the annual compensation of the first career."

More From Your Support Team

In the following case studies, observe the "sailing techniques," the trade-offs to catch more wind and stay on an even keel, the search process, and the unfolding of giftedness.

⚜

Charles D., now counselor and video producer.
When this former president of a profitable marketing company returned from his first vacation

in ten years and faced an empty future, he turned to his untapped interest—psychology.

He enrolled as a full-time student, staying two years before getting a masters in psychology and his state registration to become a marriage, family and child counselor. During that time, he supported himself and three teen-aged sons by doing minimal marketing consulting and using a small, "non-competitive" residual from his former partners.

"It was a doubtful, searching period. My sons, who lived with me and had known me as a work-aholic thought I was a dropout. I kept saying to myself, "What am I doing here? Can I really afford to do this?"

He scrambled. "I sold a condo I had on the market and that brought in just enough to pay the debts and keep us going for some months. I gave up my $25,000 auto and rode a motorcycle. Halfway through the masters program, I also remarried. In fact, I took my books to Hawaii on our honeymoon. She supported me all the way. With this new path, we were really chopped back. We can't buy furniture when we want and the kids might have to wait for braces, but there's always food on the table and the bills are paid. Ursula's son and daughter are now with us, so that means seven around the table.

"I also started, for free, a cable show which has become a series on a local community cable network. During the self-doubt period, that was another question: What am I doing this for? Indulging myself? But everything has fallen into place. Now I also do video consulting. I've put some productions together and people are paying me. So the television has evolved into some income, I've got my counseling practice, keep up some marketing consulting, and give workshops and seminars.

"From a heavy-duty achiever, I've evolved into a family man. I used to be the first one to leave the dinner table. Now I'm the last. I also run twenty-five miles a week. I have a fuller life. Not so many toys, but still a good life."

⚜

For this man, the disenchantment with one career prodded him into uncovering other giftedness. In the case of Steve C., his new "work" brought together already recognizable talents into the fulfillment of a dream.

⚜

Steve C., former freelance commercial artist and financial management consultant.

By the end of his first twenty-five years in the working world, Steve owned four businesses simultaneously: an advertising agency, an art studio, a financial management company, and a nautical gift shop. "Believe it or not, they were all connected to what I did well."

A gift for graphic design and a head for solid business management netted substantial income which, in turn, required financial management. "By the end of three years, I had learned enough about the business to begin advising others."

The nautical gift shop was the start of a boyhood dream which had also captured the enthusiasm of his wife and children. Today, he no longer owns the first three enterprises and the gift shop has been converted into a museum, with Steve serving as executive director of the non-profit California Nautical Heritage Society. His talents for finance, organization, and design have now been transferred into building the replica of a 19th-century topsail schooner. The 145-foot ship will be used as a training vessel for Sea Scouts and other interested youths.

"I'm paying back a debt. You see, for much of my childhood I lived in the outback of New Mexico. When we moved to metropolitan California, I went into culture shock and literally hid in my bedroom. Thankfully, my mom enrolled me in Sea Scouts. A string of minor successes gave me the confidence I desperately needed. From firsthand experience, I flat out know such a program can change lives.

"Sure it's a risk. We've personally invested thousands and thousands into this tall ship as well as the financial donations from others. But it's a family decision. Every family member works at the museum. We haven't risked anything except maybe creature comforts. We're like turtles, carrying everything with us, and that you can't lose.

"My hero is Thomas Jefferson, a Renaissance man. He was fascinated with architecture, agriculture, political systems, and science. I'm not afraid of variety, of learning about many things. The trick is to imitate Jefferson, be a little above average in five or six areas, and then structure something that encompasses all the areas. With the exception of the outside trappings, building and running a ship is the same as running my first four businesses."

Sometimes, the "variety of things" is not only a matter of new learning, but also a way of conducting a personal search for the "work" of one's life. And sometimes that "work" is a giftedness for doing a small task *very* well. But it might require some personal rethinking to acknowledge this fact.

The process by which Mary G. entered her own business (beginning with medical school) and the insights along the way are, I think, invaluable. Watch what role attitudes play in her search.

⚜

Mary G., manicurist in a salon catering to professionally successful and wealthy clients.

Attacking life with vigor seems to be Mary's modus operandi. She enjoyed the biochemistry challenge of her pre-med degree. Surely she'd also relish following the path of her doctor father. Two months in medical school and she changed her mind.

"I felt as if I ate, lived, and breathed medicine. You have to because the competition is so tough. I wasn't prepared to spend the next eight years starving and I began to realize that I would be married to the field. I was afraid that I'd end up fifty to sixty years old saying, 'I'm Mary G. Doctor, but what else am I? Am I happy? No, I'm a professional.' I found out that I was really going to be obsessive about it and decided that might not be the healthiest thing to do. The big thing was telling my family of my decision. My father was pretty upset."

With no idea about what she now wanted out of life, Mary decided to try a 180-degree switch. "I found the most mindless job I could think of—

a cocktail waitress. It was completely the opposite of medical school and it made great money—immediately. As I went on, I was really having fun but I caught myself lying to people. I'd say, 'Well, I'm a cocktail waitress but I have a degree.' I was justifying what I was doing.

"I finally came to grips with the fact that I was enjoying cocktailing. At the time, it was exactly what I needed and I didn't have to justify it anymore. But it was my attitude which kept saying that cocktail waitresses must be stupid. That's what I hooked on to myself. I had *assumed* all my life that anything which was in a blue-collar service meant you were a menial. That's not true. Any service can be a profession."

A lady of many talents, Mary soon added electrical wiring to her job skills. "A friend needed help wiring a video truck, and since I've always been good with my hands and had some background in electronics, I helped out. If you have any dexterity (and I was going to be a surgeon), you can pick it up. I loved it, the money was good, and there were more options in electronics than cocktailing. They offered me a full-time job and I took it."

The electronic work set her on a movie lot where the company also rented out stages. She gradually moved away from wiring into the rental office and sales. From there, it was on to a direct-mail advertising agency (one of the top three in the world) as a sales rep handling the coastal states. But not for long.

"I couldn't take the aggravation anymore. I hated going to work. I hated coming back after lunch. Even though I was good at what I did, I didn't look forward to it. I refused to spend the rest of my life in a grind.

"People told me, 'You'll never like any job. A job's a job. Period. You're not supposed to like it … you're supposed to make money at it.' That's a bunch of crap. Why can't I enjoy it?"

When her stepmother suggested manicuring, Mary looked askance. "I had this picture of a gum-snapping, blonde bimbo." The image stayed until Mary's stepmother asked her to write down answers to these questions: If you have only five years to live, what do you want to accomplish in those five years? What if you only had ninety days left? Of all the jobs you've had, what do you like most and least?

"I discovered that when all was said and done, by the time I got to the last ninety days, the travel, money, status, home, and clothes had vanished. As long as I had food on the table and liked what I was doing, that was all that mattered.

"For the second question, I decided I loved dealing with a wide variety of people, liked working with my hands, liked communicating, and the freedom to call my own hours and be my own boss."

She spent the next six months researching the field. Manicuring seemed to really add up to the list of wants and skills. Not only did Mary discover that she had a knack for it but she truly enjoyed the work. Plus, the newfound freedom from schedules allowed her to explore other areas of interest.

"But once again, I caught myself saying 'Oh, I'm a manicurist but I have a degree.' I was still hung up on the status thing. Even though I had a better time, I made more money, and I didn't have any of the headaches from before, I was still hung up on what other people thought I should be doing. Now I've gotten past that."

With the ego handled, Mary is bringing her many talents into play. "I'm going to start working with a podiatrist and doing a lecture on diabetes and the care of the feet. There's never been a manicurist who's worked with a podiatrist. I've done a thirty-minute video on doing your own home manicuring for a friend who wants to sell it to cable. Since then, I've done three "Alive and Well" shows for the Cable Health Network. The crowning touch was when I held up my feet on national television and showed everyone how to do a pedicure at home. It was fun. So I do all kinds of nutsy stuff.

"I'm getting better about time, too. At compart-mentalizing, at saying no, at prioritizing. I make time for the significant people in my life. My grand-mother used to say, 'Live fast, die young, and have a beautiful corpse.' I'd rather be old and ugly and laugh at them all."

⚜

Although these next two case studies are writers, what makes them unique in their own special way and what makes them significant for all of us is NOT what they do, but the process by which they have reached this current stage in life and the different trade-offs both have made.

⚜

Cheryl P., now freelance writer; former director of communications for a professional association.

Although miserable in her job and half-heartedly looking for another ("I didn't want to change jobs for a job's sake"), a budget cut took care of her decision to exit the "pit."

With a generous two months' severance, she decided to put money away for the mortgage and try not to panic about finding employment.

"But the more I stayed away, the more I became determined to remain my own boss; to concentrate on the stories I wanted to write; to see how long I could stay out. I'm finally starting to pursue those things that have haunted me for so long."

Although it is touch-and-go at times with the roller-coaster cycle of freelance work, Cheryl is determined to stick it out as long as possible. "I am finally paying attention to what is important to me and not what is important to someone else. Some positions took up so much time and energy that I had nothing left for me when the day was over. Why, if need be now, I could take assembly line work so that I could have a job without tremendous decisions and still have energy left over when the day was done.

"I gave up the movie channel and home delivery of bottled water. I don't buy clothes but I have leased a word processor. My parents still bring care packages, friends have me over. I'm really more conscious of a spur-of-the-moment drink or movie with friends.

"But it's good. It really makes you re-evaluate what's important in life. What you need and what you don't need. Up until now, I've just been "jobbing." Now I'm working and living. Although I made this decision some time ago, I'm also still making it. I have to keep reminding myself that this is not a passing fancy but that it *is my decision.* The struggle itself is what makes you really alive. You can't help feeling alive being this close to oblivion."

❀

There's a postscript to Cheryl's story. The irregular money from freelancing increasingly narrowed her margin for paying the most essential bills. Although she was offered other public relations positions, her very visceral reaction prompted her to turn them down. Until recently, that is. Cheryl is now employed as the community relations director for a county library system.

"I'm in a world I love and can believe in. Imagine, promoting books. I visit libraries, work with libraries, surround myself all day with words. They've even agreed to let me continue with my fiction classes. Now I can get ahead on my bills, begin to save, and use the weekends for my other writing. Whatever happens, I think I've learned there is no security. I guess your security is yourself."

❀

Richard G., playwright, former juvenile probation officer, father of seven.

A local paper once called Richard G. a "Mean Joe Green in a disgustingly sunny mood." One couldn't top that description unless it was to add "a perpetual, disgustingly sunny mood."

Apparently, he's been that way all his life. Rolling along with the tide, watching and wondering at his giftedness but not force-feeding it like a Strasbourg goose.

"When I was about seven, I decided to write a song. I knew nothing about songwriting but there I was, skipping down the street, trying to make up the words to a song. Just going down the street, singing this song. All of a sudden, I saw this man and he looked at me like I was crazy because I was really lost in what I was doing. That told me something. You could lose yourself in words. I was just out of this world, in another place.

"I did write for the high school paper and discovered that somehow I had a talent for putting what I felt down on paper. I thought everybody could do that. But mine was being published.

"I always knew I wanted to be a writer, but I got A's in Algebra. I remember my dad saying to me, 'Son, I see they're going to need ten times as many engineers in the next ten years. Do you want to be an engineer?'"

Richard tried engineering but came up against the integration of trigonometry functions. That knocked engineering out the window. But not education. At age twenty-eight he was still in college. "My goal was never to get a degree. I just kept going because it was important to me and I was enjoying it. At the same time, I worked for Rockwell as a mock-up engineer, a fancy title that didn't require an engineering degree.

"I switched into English but that only taught me about writers, not how to write. It took my first speech class to unlock the doors. I was scared to death. Knees knocking. Voice shaking. I was terrified. But the comments afterwards were so supportive. I learned a great lesson then ... what you're feeling inside isn't necessarily what you project outside."

He took more speech classes, finally transferring to another college. "I took oral interpretation and poetry. I just fell in love with that. It just started to grow inside of me. I was doing more creative writing for my speech classes than I had ever done in English."

He was still in school, taking theater courses, when he accepted a job as night supervisor at a juvenile hall. "I took the job because one of the questions asked me was if I could stay awake for long periods of time. Why, of course. That's when I would write."

Seven children later, plus a college degree at the gentle urging of a counselor who watched the number of credits climb, Richard became a probation officer. For thirteen years he continued in that role, reading his poetry to the kids in juvenile hall, self-publishing a book of poetry at the request of a University Women's Association, and writing two plays for the college.

Richard's play, "Bulldog and the Bear," struck gold. It won first place in the American College Theater Festival and as a result, was performed at Kennedy Center (with Richard in the co-lead). It has been published by Samuel French Inc., and read by James Earl Jones and Bernard Hughes for off-Broadway consideration.

"I won $5,000 for the play and took the entire family to Washington. I could've paid off all my bills and had some peace of mind, but my play was going to be performed at Kennedy Center and I wanted my kids (ages six to twenty) to see that. It was more important than any amount of money in the bank." (His entire body radiates at the memory.)

When he returned home, the reception of his writing left little doubt. "I felt the compromise with my job. Besides, my wife had been after me to quit for a couple of years. We figured I could substitute teach. We didn't know how we were going to get by over the summer, but we knew it was the right thing to do, especially with the validation. The response from the audiences told me that I was a playwright, not a probation officer.

"This is what I am supposed to be doing, therefore the conflict between my "work" and a "job" was easy to resolve—and supported by the family."

A Word About Families

Can you imagine what trouble a quarterback would have if he tried to make a touchdown without first going into a huddle with his teammates? Some might get mad and storm off the field. Others might try and play, but not knowing the game plan they would become confused and would be of zero help.

The same thing can happen with a family. Recall the medical researcher who was surprised to find out that his wife actually wanted him to seek what basically amounted to a demotion. If he had talked with her about his feelings and she had candidly shared back, the dilemma of staying in a management position might not have lasted so long.

Because a change in one area of your life impacts a change in all, dialogue is necessary. Particularly if there are children. For one thing, children fear change unless—like anyone else—they know what to expect and what role they play in that change. Even an absence of job titles can leave a child bewildered. Surprisingly, children have also learned (at way too early an age) to worry about money.

I recently met a divorced woman with a teen-aged son. When forty-plus-year-old Mom decided to leave her job as principal and seek other avenues of personal growth, her son was upset.

"I later learned that he loved telling the other kids that his mom was a principal. Without a title (I'm a management consultant), he didn't know what I did. And he was afraid we would have to move from our house." Open conversation has handled that concern, and Mom is on to more risking and growing.

The more a family can be involved in the decision-making process, even if it is in just understanding a parent's thoughts and feelings behind potential choices, there can indeed be two-way support.

A friend of mine recently left a well-paying position with a national public relations firm to start a monthly newsletter and to handle his own roster of clients. The entire family became involved in the change. They did everything from stuffing envelopes, to cleaning out the garage for his new office, to covering the phone. By playing quarterback, he's got a family team rooting for his latest adventure in growing.

Of course, let me complete this story. Before beginning his new direction, my friend played "mother" so that his wife could complete her later-in-life degree and become a CPA. Now, it's his turn.

Honest communication which leads to teamwork is the touchdown skill.

In Considering the
Eeney, Meeney, Miney, Mo

Henry Ford is credited with proclaiming, "You can't build a reputation on what you're going to do." He's right. You can't claim any freedom to live unless you lead the charge into change, monitoring balance all the while.

Additionally, there is also validity in the ancient Orthodox Jewish axiom which claims, "The gift without the giver is bare." This implies that a giver of a gift has to use it first before handing it away. The giver first cooks in the pot; first wears a shawl. Only then comes the gift-giving. Otherwise, there is nothing of the giver within the gift. It is empty.

The same thing is true of both our "work" or our "job." If we give only the minimum which is required, we'll probably get just the minimum back. The effort, therefore, is not in the quantity of our work but in the quality in which it is done and the spirit in which it is given.

By the same token, we have every right to expect reciprocation. But sometimes we've got to ask for it.

Paula works for a company that assigns clients to the respective employees. Since she has been with the firm, it has grown by leaps and bounds, literally doubling its income within two months, but adding only one new person and not hiring temporaries during vacation times.

Paula feels personally responsible for the paperwork she handles for clients and has worked weekends and nights to keep up the volume. "I suddenly realized that I was doing all the giving and not receiving anything in return. I realized that I had to speak up, stand on the quality of my work, and just see where the cards fell. I had to do it for me."

Mustering up courage, she wrote a letter, explaining her perception of the situation and unwillingness to accept such a shortage of staff. "The manager and owner walked on tiptoe after my letter, complimented my work, gave me a raise, and hired another person. That was more than I had expected! Sure it was a gamble, but now I really know that the quality of my work has paid off."

In the last three chapters, we'll look at some instances where change in the work/job picture has been forced upon individuals and how they have handled it, what are the common mental/emotional ups and downs which we all face in our growing, and lastly, how do we celebrate and live today.

Summary

1. Although multiple choices can be frightening, there are two more concepts which might provide a more well-rounded sample of possible decisions:
   – Creativity encourages you to see connections and possibilities for your work or job beyond what is a traditional path.
   – The "Road Not Taken" encourages you to consider walking a "path" which for some reason in the past was not taken.
2. The Corporate Choice can be considered with these options:
   Moving around on the inside:
   – Lateral Move (for growth of skill or a similar but different department)
   – Enrichment Move (to make your current job better)

- Exploratory Move (to try totally different fields and new skills within the same company)
- Realignment Move (to elect a downward path for more balance and personal satisfaction.)
- Relocation Move (to seek work in another company or as an entrepreneur)
- Vertical Move (to advance to a higher position and salary)

   Moving in from the outside might be considered for financial security or for balance.

   The Sit-Tight Move encourages enjoyment of current position while at the same time allows oneself to explore other interests for another time.

3. Entrepreneurial Choice:

   In all cases, feed your giftedness first and heed the wisdom of those who have gone before.

4. Before making a substantial choice, create a family team by opening communication channels.

Chapter Seven

The Timely Tragedy

— ▬ ▪ ▬ ▪ ▬ ▪ ▬ ▪ ▬ ▪ ▬ ▪ ▬ ▪ ▬ ▪ ▬ ▪ ▬ ▪ ▬ ▪ ▬ —

> Sorrow comes to make room in the heart for joy.
>
> —*The Prophet, Kahlil Gibran*

"I know a boy who grew seven inches in one year," declared a visiting friend when I was complaining about the futility of buying shoes for a growing adolescent. Noting my disbelief, she continued.

"It's true. His mother told me that one morning her son came out for breakfast complaining that he hurt all over—every joint and every muscle. He claimed he knew it was because he had grown overnight. Since his mom had measured him just the day before on a height chart hung on the inside of the linen closet door, they repeated the procedure. Sure enough—a new half an inch!"

I didn't really care whether my friend exaggerated or

not. The part of the story which struck a responsive chord in me was that the boy hurt when he grew. And the more hurt, the faster the growth.

There is no joy in being fired, going through a divorce, experiencing the death of a loved one, declaring bankruptcy, or suffering from serious illness. There is no happiness with deep disappointment or the agony of defeat. But there *is* tremendous opportunity for personal growth amid the pain.

From my experience as well as from the many people who have shared their stories, I'm convinced that such painful growing inevitably produces a fuller realization of giftedness and a more intense appreciation of living. But there is a catch. One must acknowledge, work through, and step out of that pain by actively making choices for positive growth. Otherwise, bitterness, self-pity, and eventual stagnation are the results.

I really felt a deep commitment to include this chapter. The truth of the matter is that sometimes we aren't in a "pit" until the onslaught of a seemingly terrible event that kicks us out of the proverbial catbird seat. In other instances, we might be aware of an unhappy or imbalanced work/life but we don't spring into action until we're forced to. If there was ever a time when you needed to know that others had indeed passed through and triumphed, it is now. Hence this chapter.

Were it not for a budget cut and two months' severance pay, Cheryl's dream of working as a freelance writer and creating fiction stories would have had reality only in midnight slumber. Were it not for the cancellation of his English teaching job and the discovery that his separated wife had a new beau, William Least Heat Moon would never have traveled those forgotten American roads and produced his best-seller *Blue Highways*. Charles D.'s catalyst for finally walking away from his company came because he watched his father die. "I realized that he had never had any fun or time off in his life. I didn't want my life to end like that." Even broadcaster/author Studs Terkel observed that were it not for a lucky set of circumstances, he would have been an admittedly unhappy lawyer: He flunked the bar exam.

Although each probably entered a state of depression or at least a blue funk over the event, none of them remained there. When one door closed, they chose to open another. Sometimes, one doesn't even know what's on the other side of the new door. Case in point:

Some five years ago, my then-soon-to-be husband invested considerable money and time into seeking a contract which would have moved us out of the state. I was ecstatic because if he won the contract, I was to leave my job as a senior account executive with a public relations firm and become the director of communications for a 200-person project. What a challenge! What an opportunity to put together everything from written materials to employee relations programs!

A week after we were married, word came back. "Sorry. You didn't make it." The door which we had both dreamed about slammed shut with the finality of a bank vault. Only I had my foot caught.

It took but a few weeks of deep depression, frustration, headaches and tears to realize that I had been using Bill's project as a way to get out of a situation which no longer matched the "me" I was becoming. Instead of making a choice for myself, I had tried to let "circumstance" do it for me.

And our circumstances seemed sticky: three stepchildren soon to be living with us, Bill's consulting work in a slump from his single-devotion to the contract proposal, and a "pit" for me. At face value, the resultant downside from the risk of seeking the contract looked too steep.

Yet with Bill's encouragement, I left the secure world of a monthly paycheck. Today, thanks to that timely tragedy, I am beginning to discover giftedness which I never knew I had. And he has developed a management concept unique to his profession.

You've Been Fired

When you read the heading of this section, do you wince? Feel ill at ease? I did. Just those words alone are a real downer. The connotation behind "getting fired," whether it's for budget cutbacks or just plain unsuitability for the job, is that you are not worthy. The downsizing of the last half of this decade has reached record numbers. In the scheme of things, you can be replaced. And the higher up in salary and rank, the more traumatic the termination.

Turning the traumatic into opportunity is what Bill Ellermeyer knows best. As president of Career Management Services, a former firm now sold to a large outplacement corporation, he has firsthand knowledge of the displaced executive and what it takes to regroup and unfold after a termination.

"When I was forty-two, I got lucky. I was fired."

Now sitting in his office years after that timely tragedy, Bill references the unfolding process in his "work," the resultant success of his company, and what his clients have discovered about themselves.

"I was vice president of personnel for a major transportation carrier at the time I was asked to leave. But for sometime I realized that the title really should have been 'labor relations.' I was the classic case of the misfit."

The company gave him five months to look at what he wanted, "and for the first time in my lie, that's exactly what I did."

"With the help of a process supplied by some consultants, I looked at myself and discovered things I never considered before. First, since about the age of ten, it seems like I have been a natural counselor for my family, for school friends, and for my colleagues at work. Counseling is a streak that runs through my life like a thread."

"The second thing I found out was that I was something of a performer. I liked to get up before a group. I never did stand-up presentations in my work, but the talent was there on the inside. I also realized that I had the ability to put myself in the other guy's shoes, to have empathy.

"What this showed me was that my skills were dealing on a one-to-one basis with others. The top job in personnel within the corporation involves managing, planning, and organizing—taking me away from what I was best at doing. My skills are interpersonal, performing, training, and speaking.

"Half of me said 'Go out on your own.' The other half said 'What, are you kidding? After twenty years of getting a paycheck!'

"But that's what I did; I didn't know what my inherent skills were until I was forty-two years old. I also discovered that I was a risk-taker and that I like change. So here I am."

According to Bill, the average profile of the outplaced executive whom he counsels is a forty-six-year-old executive, making $90,000 to $150,000 per year, with a company tenure of about ten years. The corporate reason for

firing the executive might be one or all of the following:
1. A misfit. (This is a talented person who just gets into the wrong kind of job.)
2. Personality clash. (A new man or woman who regularly runs into conflict with senior management.)
3. Economic cutbacks.
4. The Redundant Executive. (The man or woman has moved ahead into a position that really carries no definition or responsibility. And there they stay as a figurehead.)
5. "Downsizing" to meet global competition.

Regardless of the corporate rationale, Bill has discovered that all of his displaced executives were really unhappy to begin with.

"I don't think there is anyone who has come in to see us who didn't have some sense of being miserable in his or her job. That's why getting fired can really be the key to opportunity. Many people don't like what they are doing but won't make an effort to change because they like getting the paycheck ... they don't want to ripple the waters. They're in neutral, without vibrancy, just coasting. Many just think about it through their entire careers. Some are so anxious about their job insecurity, they've become immobile and have not taken responsibility for their own careers. I've done retirement counseling and heard people say, 'Well, this is what I've done and I really hated it but the social aspects (lunches, friends, etc.) kept me going.'

Sure you hear a lot about middle managers getting axed and how tragic it is. But in many ways, that's going to change their lives in a positive way. Most people don't want to look at themselves, to open the door. But when you're fired, you're forced to. You have to take responsibility for yourself. The crutch is gone."

In looking back over their achievements and what energized them, the terminated executives learn how to talk about themselves and what skills they bring to the world.

"People get defined according to their jobs and job descriptions are very narrow. Even if someone doesn't like being an engineer, ask who they are and they'll say 'an engineer.' So very early on, you get a label and don't know that it's just an invisible piece of paper that can come off at will. You don't know that you have tremendous powers and abilities far bigger than any job."

Once realization of inherent abilities sets in—even if triggered by losing a job—the process of unfolding must continue. Bill admits he's feeling the tug of still-untapped skills. "I feel like I'm moving toward more speaking, performing, and seminars. There is much information which I can share so I've joined the National Speakers Association. It might also balance the intense work I do and give me more time at home with my wife and our new, first-and-only-child."

A Sidebar About Balance

Because "you're fired"—for whatever reason—reverberates through the inner soul as "you're incompetent," there's a tendency to want to prove to everyone else, including yourself, that you can make it in the world of work. It becomes mighty easy to plunge into the next position or, as Bill did, into an entrepreneurial spot and attack it with all the gusto you've got.

That's fine to a point. However, put undivided attention into the intellectual or work area of your life for an extended length of time and the connections with "living" begin to weaken.

This time, Bill serves as my case study instead of my resource.

&

Bill E., ex-president, outplacement firm.

"The imbalance started when the company grew extensively the first year and I had four people working for me. Now, from a standpoint of running a business, I realize I didn't need that many. It just created an extra burden for me. I was producing the work and feeding them, but no one was developing the business.

"I guess I also thought that an increased size would give visibility to the firm and that it would have some momentum by itself when I wasn't here. I feel much better, less pressured, more calm now that I only bring in help when I need it.

"But I'm still so wrapped up in business. I don't seem to enjoy myself as much as I would like or have any time for fun. I read too much about business matters and I guess I think I don't deserve to have any fun. Ever since I've been in business, I've stopped the play I like—water skiing, traveling, time for the family, and relaxation. I have guilt feelings about not taking time for the spiritual, too— the inner me. Right now, I only go 'inside' in a crisis.

"However I'm making progress. I'm more relaxed because I changed the structure of my company. At least I know what's wrong."

&

"Sailing" never stops, does it?

When the Spouse Has Gone

I have to place the blame at the feet of society for what I am about to write. I didn't make it up. It's a matter of sociological happenstance: Divorce or the death of a spouse carries more severe impact in the work/job arena for women than for men.

Of all the divorced people you know, how many women have received such a gracious settlement that they do *not* have to work? Not very many out of the total picture, hmm? And yet, how many of those women (1) never had a job, (2) have a job but with a salary much lower than the former husband, (3) have custody of the children.

Now think about divorced men and answer those same questions, substituting the word "wife" for "husband" in question two. Do you see the difference?

I had to ask myself these questions when I began compiling case studies for this chapter. As I searched and asked for potential people to interview, it appeared that more men grew in their "work" through the tragedy of job termination whereas more women grew in their "work" through divorce or death of a spouse. The Bureau of Labor Statistics confirmed at least part of my supposition: Based on the 1990 census, men's income after divorce rose whereas women's income declined.

Sure, there are exceptions. I personally know of one case where the ex-wife took the husband to the cleaners and he is faced with starting all over again from scratch. And, thankfully, there is a slow and good change in the court philosophy which has more equitably divided the responsibility for child-rearing.

But in general, you can see why more divorced or widowed women would have a greater likelihood to encounter "work" with more trauma than men. And if a woman has never worked, hopefully you can appreciate her tremendous difficulty and therefore potential in discovering her giftedness.

According to Elaine Hart, former director of The Women's Opportunity Center, a University of California, Irvine, non-profit prototype career and personal counseling service for community members, the center has seen more than 80,000 individuals stream through its doors since 1970, most because of divorce or death.

"A number of the women we see are the products of an affluent life. They've been married to movers and shakers, contenting themselves with a 'devoted wife' role. Suddenly, they're left without an identity, and frequently, without much income. They see themselves as unskilled, incapable, and futureless," says Hart. "We assist them in going through a process to identify and tap hidden knowledge and skills. I can readily say that most of our clients discover potential which they never thought they had. Before they had allowed themselves to be smothered. Now divorce has become the best thing in the world for them."

A few examples: One divorcee is a well-known former actress in her fifties. She never completed high school and has always been surrounded by servants. Now faced with a much different future, she's returning to get her degree and is getting excited over new possibilities.

On the other end of the spectrum, another woman had lost everything, including a place to stay. She slept in her station wagon. When she'd come into our Center's Job Seekers Clinic, we always were surprised to see how professionally dressed she appeared. Someone complimented her clothing, only to learn that each outfit had been carefully orchestrated with penny-pinching wisdom from a local thrift store. The important point here is that she began to reframe the way she saw herself. She now has a good job working with doctors."

Sometimes, the divorced or widowed woman must unfold gradually. When Joyce (fictitious name) entered the doors of the Job Seekers Clinic she could not give a positive statement about herself, her self-esteem was down the drain, and her skills (to her way of thinking) were negligible. A series of smaller jobs began to boost her confidence and allow her to discover more about herself. Today, she's one of the top sales representatives for a manufacturer of pharmaceutical supplies.

Not all women, or men for that matter, have such resources as the Center available to them. But even without that assistance, those who successfully move through divorce and into a growing work/life balance have managed to first tap into their giftedness. Although both women in the following case studies started their personal journeys with divorces, their stories contain universal messages about risk and gain, balance and "work."

⚜

Marsha P. (fictitious name), director of private pre-school and elementary school.

When she's on the playground with her three-year-old students, Marsha moves to a different beat. She's no longer forty-seven years old with three almost grown-up sons, but a youngster—giggling, playing ball, pretending.

There are 250 children in her school and she knows each by name. It's easy when teaching and loving children for their special individuality is a heartfelt philosophy.

But Marsha almost kept that gift under wraps. "Although I taught five years before my first son was born, I quit as soon as he came. The culture said that a good wife and mother didn't work. That's what I believed in. So instead, I helped Tom get his business started. I even wrote his dissertation for him."

For thirteen years, Marsha played at housewife, mother *and* father. More often than not, Tom traveled during the week and was too tired to notice either his sons or his wife.

"I really wanted to get back with children and other adults. Tom didn't know it, and wouldn't have approved, but I volunteered for an inner-city Head Start program where I could take my boys along with me. They were the only towheads in the group!"

The older Marsha got, the more unhappy she became. Tom told her that she was being foolish to ask for repeated signs of affection and more "at-home time." Finally, at the age of thirty-six, her marriage had deteriorated to such a state that Tom, in a fit of anger, threw Marsha and the boys out of the house.

"What a scary, frightening experience. For two weeks, the boys and I lived in a motel until I could find a job at a pre-school. I could take the two youngest with me and drop my other son at elementary school. Tom refused to give me any money and the job provided just enough for a small apartment and food for us."

Although her husband finally relented and allowed them to return, the marriage was over. "I accepted a position as the director of a church-related school in order to be home when the boys got out of school. It was like having your cake and eating it too."

Having subsequently enrolled in a masters program at a university in the next county, Marsha continued to refine her teaching skills and philosophy. "I realized that the idea of mainstreaming special-needs children within a regular classroom was something that could not wait until elementary school. But when I tried it at the church school, the board members balked."

Up against a wall, Marsha took a deep breath, sold her share of stock from the divorce settlement, and started a private school where she could provide more individualized learning and encourage early admittance of handicapped youngsters.

That was nineteen years ago. Today, the school that started with forty-five preschoolers now goes up to grade six and the woman who had never thought further than marriage and babies now deals with corporate board members, employees, and accountants. "And I got my degree, even if it took me seven years and a 100-mile round-trip commute."

There's a man back in her life, whitewater raft trips, aerobics classes, a bevy of friends from all walks of life, and an avid interest in holistic health. Recently, she sold the school to start another career.

⚜

Do you remember Sunny F., the woman from Chapter One who headed out to California with her teen-aged daughter, $1,500 to her name, and a "maybe" job in the wings? Seven years later, at age fifty-four, her writing started to roll: a book on archery for the Olympics, a script sold to network television, teachers' guides and filmstrips for Disney, a radio telethon for a national charity campaign, a teleconference script on agriculture for a bank in the Midwest, and a movie-of-the-week script currently under consideration. Quite an accomplishment for a lady who didn't begin unfolding until the end of a twenty-year marriage.

Sunny, F., writer for business, industry, and television.

"Leaving my marriage, at the age of forty-two, was the first time I ever took control of my life. Ever. Up until then I had allowed myself to be pushed and manipulated into everything. My life had always been in other people's hands because I had to please everyone. I had to be loved and the only way to be loved was to be the person everyone wants you to be. I got so lost in being a person for someone else, I never found out who I was.

"Deciding to seek a divorce was the most painful decision. I had what I called a mini-breakdown, crying at the tiniest things all the time. Things were happening in my life which I would ignore until I became physically sick. There was no one I could talk to because everyone thought I had a perfect marriage; I was the perfect wife, the perfect mother. When the doctor couldn't find a damn thing wrong with me, I got scared and realized I had to make a decision.

"I started writing because I could do it at home and be a good mother. We really needed the money.

Wherever we had moved in the past, I would call on public relations and advertising agencies even though at first I hadn't done that type of writing. My college degree is in speech therapy."

But Sunny was scared. "I didn't really believe in my own talent or ability. Confidence level was zero. I never thought of myself as begin able to be really good at writing. At that time in my life, I knew I loved to write but...."

Within short order, another crisis. The production company closed its doors, the little money she had was gone, a daughter still had to be fed and there were no jobs in the small town.

When there's no road in sight, some people seek counselors. Sunny sought a psychic. "She insisted that I was going to work at a university in the northern part of the state—a crazy notion since I don't have a masters—and go back to school. I told her that was ridiculous. I didn't have two cents and what money I did have for school was to help my daughter with college."

In less than a week, a casual acquaintance called to ask if she would consider applying for an adjunct teaching position in a university school of journalism!

"I didn't have any journalism training, though I had done a house magazine for a national hamburger chain. I knew nothing about printing and yet there I was, talking to the dean of the school. I had never taught, but I knew I would love it; daydreamed about it. But without a masters, it all seemed so impossible."

The impossible did occur. When the dean heard

about her background in film, Sunny was sent
directly to the chairman of the broadcasting department who also served as the general manager of the
university's public television station. A $9,000 per
year job was available doing public relations for the
station. "I knew I couldn't live on that, but what
choice did I have?"

After a two-hour interview, the chairman
became her mentor. "He tore up the application from
another person and sent me down to apply for the
public relations job. He also told me to hang loose
about a part-time teaching position.

Patience paid off. He got a waiver for her to
teach despite the missing master's degree. On and
off for the next three years she taught, learning just
ahead of the students. "I was asked to take over a
newswriting lab. Never having written that format, I
studied the material and taught the lab. A student
was sent to me so that I could teach her how to write
a screenplay. So I learned how to write a screenplay."

While teaching the newswriting lab, a documen-
tary film on a Presbyterian hunger project sent her to
Bangladesh. (She had done a similar project in
Brazil a few years earlier.)

"Up until that time, I still didn't believe I was
really any good. I didn't believe I had value. But I
found myself halfway across the world and loving
every minute of it. People's reaction when they
heard of my work convinced me—not because the
film was the greatest, but because I had been called
twice to go overseas. That says something. I was not
just getting these things because I was cheap and

needed the money. People were beginning to treat me with respect. It changed my attitude about myself."

It was then that Sunny decided she wanted to be a star ... "and that I always wanted to be a star ever since I was growing up. I remember being on stage toe dancing, music playing, and people applauding. I loved it, simply loved it.

"This 'stardom' I wanted now was not being in the spotlight, but being recognized for my craft. Being so good that people will use my name in reference to good writers. At age forty-five, that all became rekindled. I didn't just want to be a college professor and survive. I wanted to be such a damn successful writer that I'd be invited back to teach, maybe even awarded an honorary doctorate. I love working with talent and pulling it out, but I didn't want to be a news teacher doing the same course year after year. With all my heart and soul I wanted to do dramatic writing."

It hasn't been easy. The risks remain but the giftedness that began unfolding with a divorce has attracted a sense of happiness and well-being.

"When I look back, I don't even know who that woman is from my past life. I felt like a caterpillar until I went to the university. Then I became a butterfly. It gave me a chance to find out that I could make it on my own after twenty years. It built courage. Before then, I was never fully me. I did a lot of nice things, even wrote a musical which was very successful, but I never related those things to who I was. Now I relate who I am to what I do."

You've Lost Your Business

Some married friends of ours are currently engaged in a critical struggle to keep open what once was a very profitable company that rebuilt engines for trucks. Unexpected debt from buying out a partner, a too-soon expansion move, and poor management has placed them in a position where Chapter 11 bankruptcy might be the only solution.

"So if that's what happens, and we sell the house, we'll still be all right. We've got each other and our health." With an attitude like that and some of the fine help they've acquired, they are confident that they'll make it. But some people aren't so lucky.

When losing a business does strike, two opportunities can result from the tragedy. The first is balance and a resetting of priorities. Not infrequently, an enterprise fails because too much money was taken out of the business to handle choices in other life areas or too little attention was paid to the business of management. In these cases, a "clean slate" might allow an individual to reorganize "living" and "working" in a more manageable fashion. Ultimately, that must be a plus.

But the greater opportunity which might lay buried underneath such a tragedy is a newfound freedom to really explore and find one's true "work." In this trial-and-error process of figuring out just who we are and how we want to be, there's a pretty good chance that the lost business is merely a detour in our journey.

❦

Such was the case with Martin W. (fictitious name), who at the time I first met him, was president

*of a graphic design studio with gross annual billings
around $600,000.*

When I first walked into Martin's graphic design
studio, this boyish-looking commercial artist was
completing the final touches on a packaging idea for
a pharmaceutical house. Three other employees
seemed intently involved in their specific assignments for a stable of clients which included a large
biomedical firm and an auto manufacturer. Wife
Susan manned the reception desk, waiting until it
was time to go home to their two children.

At first glance, it appeared like any other graphic
studio. Until, that is, Martin gave me a tour.

Behind his desk on the second floor was a small
door. When I inquired as to that space, Martin
allowed me to enter a room under the eaves of the
building. A great winged owl glared at me from its
rough pine tree perch; deer nuzzled gentle spring
grass; and a massive gray whale glided through
watery light filtered between bands of blue-green
crystal and velvet. All as alive as if I were the
original Creator. All captured within a world no
bigger than a picture frame.

Martin's business sign might have read
"commercial artist" but here was his true gift—fine
arts illustration of wildlife.

"But why aren't you doing this," I gasped
reaching out to touch the paper, feel the paint, and
make sure that it wasn't a very artistic photograph.
"Too busy," answered Martin, hurrying into the next
room but not before he sighed. "I work on this at
home in the garage but I rarely have the time. I don't
have the credentials to do this for a living.

Commercial art supports us."

End of conversation. And after three months, end of the project which had mutually used our skills. I heard no more from Martin for almost three years until the bottom fell out and he called me.

"I always felt rather inept at running the business. I couldn't manage people very well and I'm afraid it was easy for Sue and I to be taken advantage of. We were talked into incorporating more as a protection against personal liability since we handled drug and medical accounts. However, unknown to us, the accountant continued to file our tax return as if we were sole proprietors."

Martin didn't know about the error until a state tax official walked up the driveway to his home and handed him a bill for some $8,000 in unpaid corporate taxes and penalties. The agency agreed to accept an initial minimum payment of $1,000 per week for eight weeks. (Later, the IRS requirement would bring the total amount to almost $32,000!)

"We scrambled like hell and immediately sold what we could. But now there was an even bigger nut to crack. A graphic designer has heavy out-of-pocket expenses until the client can be billed. We sold some of the office furniture and cut back on employees."

When the fourth week came around, Martin missed the payment deadline by one day. The state tax agency instantly seized all personal accounts. "Only later did we learn that the agency acted improperly but that it would take more money and probably four years to handle any litigation. Besides, on that day—it made little difference.

"Our house payment was due and the only money we had was in my pocket and Sue's purse. That same day, a letter arrived from a major client on retainer, picking up on the 30-day cancellation clause in the contract."

Susan went back to work as an office manager for a doctor, Martin closed shop and moved his commercial art home. "We lived off of everything in the pantry while I used the checks from clients to pay bills. I pounded the streets, hit and miss. It felt like a giant roller coaster. I'd get enough work to support the family and then, whoosh! Down in the valley."

In retrospect, the valley created by this tragedy provided Martin with the time and drive to unleash his creative genius. "I painted my brains out and spent much of the time meeting the scientific community, museum curators, marine biologists, and ornithologists. I even met with a major environmental group and had a whale painting ready to be turned into a poster when the funding was cut."

To earn more money, Martin located a gallery specializing in wildlife. Though the interior of the gallery provided a gorgeous backdrop for his work, its location next to a shopping center proved disastrous.

"But through the gallery, I met other wildlife artists. One of them, who was among the original members of Greenpeace, invited me to display my work at the Mendocino County Whale Festival in Northern California.

"After having my ego take such a blow, wondering how I could have been so stupid to have fallen into the trap of the big office, I felt re-confirmed by the Mendocino artists. One artist whom I had read so much about and greatly admired came to my display at the festival. He stood for over an hour looking at my work like a kid in a candy store—the same way I felt about his talent. The next day, he returned with a camera and asked permission to photograph it."

At the end of one week in Mendocino County, Susan and Martin looked at each other, thought about the metropolitan rat race and said, "Why not! We're selling our house to pay the state, and the IRS will soon be along. Rent is cheaper in this area but most of all, there are people here who will help support my work. They're our kind—real people without pretense and show. Considering the fact that I sold a number of paintings during the festival, it seems that the area is also visited by people who appreciate wildlife artistry."

The wheels are now in motion for such a move and a new life. All because of a seeming tragedy.

A PotpouRRí oƒ MísƒoRtune

I have purposely selected those timely tragedies which appear to have universal recognition for many of us. This doesn't exclude the fact there may be any number of events which hit us below the belt, force us into action, and encourage a rethinking of our personal journey and ideas for happiness.

Elaine Hart the former director of the Women's Opportunity Center, became bedridden for over a year with crippling arthritis. With plenty of time to think, she realized that her life spent in nurturing a family had helped them, but still left her with a feeling of wanting more. This strong-spirited woman overcame the debilitating illness and returned to college for her masters in counseling. Her subsequent work with the center has touched the lives of many.

Luke (fictitious name), a former Philadelphia sales executive continues each day to conquer the disease of alcoholism. "I learned to live at higher and higher levels of pain before I admitted my illness." Although he has lost his job in the process of treatment, the sales executive facade is beginning to crack. The real Luke has the first real chance in years to emerge ... and with that emergence will come true working and living.

What Does It All Mean?

It means that sometimes we have to be thrown overboard before we can begin to make the choices that will allow us to truly be free to live.

But it also means that while there may be grief and mourning, sorrow and self-doubt, we'll never clamber back into the boat unless we reach for the gunwale and pull ourselves in.

It might be helpful to think of such an event in this frame of reference. A local minister once drew a dot within the middle of a large sheet of white paper. When he asked the congregation just what they saw, the answer came back loud and strong, "A black dot."

"Ah yes," he nodded sadly. "Did none of you see the white paper ... the *big* white sheet of paper that stretches well beyond this little dot?

"Your narrow focus on what is actually a very small, rather ugly speck on a much larger field of clean paper demonstrates just what happens when you channel all your energies and attention on a single unhappy or tragic event. The world and possibilities for happiness are truly much greater than you have recognized."

Summary

1. A timely tragedy is one in which we are forced to deal with choices for our "work" and living.
2. The manner in which we allow ourselves to explore and expand our giftedness determines, to a great extent, just how fast we can move through and out of the timely tragedy.

Chapter Eight

Uppers, Downers and In-Betweeners

—————————————————————

Life is, without question, a fluid changing
process in which nothing is permanent or fixed.
—*Carl Rogers*

Just last week we returned from ten days backpacking
in the High Sierras, an annual family jaunt that had this
flatland-bred lady scrambling over boulders, puffing up
mountain passes, wading across turbulent snow-fed creeks,
and counting shooting stars that whisk across a crowded
night sky. When you're sleeping 11,000 feet above sea
level, even new galaxies appear.

It occurred to me that this experience resembles, in
many ways, the process of working and living. The trail
carried me up peaks, down into valleys, across plateaus.
Sometimes I stayed in one place longer than another, but
eventually I had to move on. When it came time to thread

our way up switchbacks, I knew that my water bottle better be filled and my walking stick in hand. Although each mountain pass was different, at least I was prepared.

That's the reason I felt a need for this chapter. In the process of making choices for balance and work/life, we all can expect to emotionally walk up, down, and across. BUT, if we know in advance that such movement is a natural part of the process, we might be better prepared for the road. Secondly, it might also be helpful to understand (and hopefully cultivate) some of the personal mindsets which appear to promote quality working and living.

Let's first look at what emotions we might encounter in making choices for being faithful to our giftedness, our "work."

Emotions

Fear of Failure

It appears to me that there are two types of fear: pre-decision and post-decision. The first one keeps us nailed to the floor saying, "I can't." The second one keeps us running around in circles mumbling over and over again, "Oh #S%&%%. What have I done?!" And both leave us depressed.

I spent about a year holding off writing a query letter to a publisher because I was afraid. Once I worked up enough courage to put my idea out for inspection, I was then faced with a signed contract and more fear. In fact, I probably wrote five drafts of the first chapter because I couldn't force myself to move into the book. Afraid again. Afraid that I couldn't cut the mustard, that I would be a failure. Oh, I didn't figure out what I was doing to myself for a while. I thought that it was just because I was too busy with my other work to find time to conduct interviews, to do the research and begin writing.

And then it hit. I was choosing to accept assignments rather than getting down to the real task at hand. I discovered that while I had successfully controlled (not cancelled out) fear in the past, this was a bigger risk for me. As John Powell points out in his book, *Fully Human, Fully Alive,* I was holding on to some attitudes about myself which needed to be discarded: Everyone must like what I do or I am not acceptable.

Because I hadn't seen this attitude creep into my other work where I regularly face the public, deep inside I realized the tremendous personal importance of this book. Once I understood what I was doing to myself, I took steps to rearrange my thinking. I wrote affirmation cards that countered my old attitude. I turned down other work and cleared the decks for the book. And I took a deep breath and started—this time with real joy and renewed conviction.

Fear of failure might also keep us back from making choices for balance. Certainly fear is a primary emotion keeping Dr. O'Donnell and his fellow physicians from screaming "no more" to the unrealistic demands of a workload which takes every ounce of stamina.

Stephanie (fictitious name) is part of the senior management team in a powerful conglomerate. Taking her cue from her workaholic boss, she continues to carry home a briefcase filled to the brim with reports, rises before the sun is up to keep herself no less than two weeks behind schedule, and admits to doing the work of two or three people. Not only that, but she also sits on the board of non-profit groups, attempts to make time for her lover and friends, and then crumples into exhaustion or nervous palpitations.

When asked why she doesn't call a halt somewhere, she says "I can't. Everybody has to work this way." But think about this: As it is used here, the word "can't" really only holds two realities. Either "I don't know how to do it" or "I'm afraid to do it."

In the first instance, until one attempts to do something, one really doesn't know if he/she can or cannot accomplish a task. Since there is rarely only one solution to a problem, one must attempt to take numerous actions before accurately saying, "I can't."

In the second instance, fear enters the picture. And how often haven't we also heard people compound the problem by adding, "I'm the only one who can do this work."

Maybe that's so. In which case, only Stephanie can control the workload by either trying out various solutions or by really looking at her fear and what attitudes lie beneath the surface.

But in most cases, we are not the only ones who can do the work. We might be the only ones who can do it in our particular manner, in our particular time frame, but there are others available for help. The thought of giving up some of our work to others might be threatening to our self-concept as powerful, fully capable people. The opposite is actually true. Giving up work which others might do actually empowers us to expand into other activities which are suited to our individual talents.

Fear of Success

There's an equally common fear which is the exact opposite of what I experienced. The yang to the yin of failure is the fear of success. It is probably one of the most talked-about, read-about fears currently in the public eye.

As I see it, the core of this fear is a sense that with success comes lack of control, an imbalance, an upsetting of the apple cart when it comes to relationships, lifestyle, and maybe even personal values. The person grappling with this fear actually personifies "The Success" and gives it power to control his/her life.

Notice the verb "give." We only lose control when we choose to see ourselves as helplessly manipulated rather than being the manipulators.

What to Do About It

> Worry is interest paid on a debt you might not owe.
>
> – William Inge

In reflecting about fear of failure and success, and considering my experience, I'm convinced once again that fear is made from a two-step recipe. The first ingredient is a crystal ball. The second is an attitude coated with feelings.

The crystal ball comes from our imagination where we project what might happen if we make a certain choice. Hours and hours of worry are spent anticipating something that might never happen. We look negatively and fearfully into the future.

We experience a feeling when we contemplate that imagined future. The deeper question which must be asked is this: What am I telling myself that is creating my response? Is this attitude, my perception of reality, something which is valid or is it time to change?

Fear can also be a good thing. Without fear we'd leap from buildings, walk across a burning tar pit, and jeopardize our well-being and maybe even that of others. As Benjamin

- -

Disraeli insisted, "Next to knowing when to seize an opportunity, the most important thing in life is to know when to
forgo an adventure."

That's why it becomes terribly important to really
challenge fear and test its true mettle. You might even luck
out, as I did, and gain a new insight and a freeing attitude.

Like pits, fear comes in a variety of intensities ranging
from mild worries to full-on phobias, the latter which
requires professional assistance. But for our purposes, may
I share some general techniques which either I've found
personally useful or which others have used. And we'll also
turn to our case studies for more insight.

Visualization

Mentally put yourself in the situation you fear, and
this time imagine that you are really coping with it and
maybe even enjoying it. (I visualized myself wrapping the
book for a Christmas present; speaking from a podium and
laughing with the audience; receiving letters from readers.)

Jump Right In

Expose yourself, if possible, to that which you fear
until you get over it. (I went to my office at 7:00 a.m.,
turned on the computer, and just plain began writing.)

Worst Case

This is one of my favorite ones. I ask myself, "What
would be the worst thing that could happen." Almost
inevitably I realize that the "worst" case is actually not all
that bad and I could handle it. Besides, I'd learn from the
experience.

Reality Testing

Ask yourself if there is ample, real proof that whatever you fear might occur. (For example, I've never heard of an author getting hanged because some readers didn't like a book.) Make sure that you honestly assess the similarity between your situation and the test case. Ask an impartial third party to listen to your comparison for its validity.

Get Away From It

Sometimes fear or worry can so clog the mental processes that nothing moves through it. Switch channels into something else like exercise, sleep, gardening, painting, reading, yoga, or whatever else might be your brain's Drano.

Comedy Capers

A sense of humor is really nothing more than a sense of perspective—clear, wide-angle perspective which allows us to rejoice in laughter at our own fallibility and that of others. Certainly Norman Cousins' now-famous illness must have initially carried tremendous fear with it—fear which he mitigated through humor. Even Lincoln is credited with this proclamation: "With the fearful strain that is on me night and day, if I did not laugh I should die."

Worry "Things"

This might be considered a way of combining a number of these techniques—everything from visualization to humor. Basically it implies that you put your fear or worry someplace else, that you move it out of your head and give it shape and form. I've seen people write the name of their fear on a rock and then throw it away. Others might draw their fear (probably getting a good belly laugh in the process) and then either burn the paper, or stick it away for another time. I've even seen worry dolls from Guatemala. These tiny figures, male and female, fit inside a small box and can be readily christened with the title of any fear or worry you wish.

By moving the fear into a place where you look at it, you regain control and perspective.

Choices and Depression

Since this chapter is designed to prepare you for what you might experience, we do need to be aware that a significant work move cannot be made without evoking depression—here defined as loss, ambivalence, and of course, fear that things just won't work out. The longer you were with an organization, the closer your ties with fellow employees, the greater will be your sense of loss. Depending upon just what that new work choice is, you might also feel rootless, detached, and without direction.

Every time we leave something behind, we experience loss—and all loss must be mourned. If we take a clue from the hospice movement, words are necessary to dissipate sorrow. You must talk about the experience with people who can empathize without intrusion.

Depression might also come because our choices have not lived up to our expectations. True to form, the crystal ball and our imagination have done a number on us. It's time once again to try reality testing on our expectations and also to examine what might be that feeling-covered attitude. If I uncover an unrealistic expectation, my depression has no reason for being.

FoR MoRe SuppoRt With FeaR, DepRession anꝺ Choices

Whenever we chance to meet other backpackers on the trail, it is customary to exchange information about what lies ahead. There's much support and understanding in sharing mutual experiences. One is no longer alone. In fact, I'm glad to see other people looking as haggard as I do. Then I realize it's all part of the journey.

This brief collection of case studies is offered with the same spirit.

⚜

Sandy R., salesperson of industrial couplings.

"The hardest decision I ever made was to leave teaching. I knew once I hopped out, I couldn't hop back. My confidence was very shaky and I was petrified. I think I just held my nose and jumped. And I became depressed after I left because the training program at my company didn't keep me busy enough. I was in limbo. Since I was following other salespeople around, I didn't have customers of my own and had no way of measuring my progress. In fact, I was laid off twice during the first year. The first time I was scared and the second time I was angry. But I stuck it out.

"I handle depression by giving in to it. I get it out of my system by wallowing in it: listening to the saddest music, crying all I want, and jogging. Then it vanishes.

"I've learned much in this process. Change is growth and anytime you move into the unknown you grow. The more self-knowledge you have, the more you have to give. Allowing yourself to grow in business and personal life is the only way you can say 'This is who I am.'"

⁂

Cheryl P., public relations administrator and freelance writer.

Once she determined to support herself with writing, Cheryl made adjustments in her lifestyle so as to lower the monthly income requirement. "But some days you think you're going to lose it all.

"But I keep going back to the fact that this is not a passing fancy but *my decision.* I'm doing it for myself. Sometimes, I laugh about fear and depression. I give myself mental pep talks, reminding myself that it's all worth the risk. It's something I've wanted for a long time.

"When I'm down, I tell myself that it's temporary, that it'll pass and it always does. And there's just not enough one can say about good friends, people who support, encourage and are just there for laughs, for counseling, even for objectivity.

"I figure that the worst which might happen is that I'll sell the house. Big deal. Besides [she laughs], I'd make a good waitress."

⁂

Bill E., former president of Career Management Services.

"After I was fired and opened my practice, I went to experiential workshops, meditation courses, positive affirmation courses—just a whole lot of things. It was lonely. That's why I selected an executive suite with other professionals and became involved in professional organizations. I needed the socialization.

"I was afraid of failure, financial insecurity. I didn't think I could take not getting a weekly paycheck. But building up a support network of other consultants helped considerably."

❧

Charles D., counselor and video producer.

"I hang in there, get through the anxiety and do it. It's been that kind of a process. I've been like a cat on a hot tin roof. Are people going to buy my services as a consultant? Am I going to make it as a psychologist?

"Oh yes. Change is fearful. I always have fear with me but I've learned not to let it take control. When I recognize the signs, I talk to myself. 'Hi, fear. So you're going to be here awhile. Well, hang on while I do some self-affirmations.' I answer the fear back."

❧

For Sunny F., now age sixty, a multitude of fears arose around the time she made her crucial decision to leave the university and become a screenwriter.

"In my forty-fifth year, I was offered a chance to go to Bangladesh and write a documentary. I left, fully convinced that I would be dead within the year. You see, both parents died at forty-five. That was traumatic. I lived in a house in my teens where when you came home, you never knew if your father was going to be alive or dead.

"I returned on my forty-fifth birthday, certain

that I had cancer. Instead, what I did have was a parasite from Bangladesh. When I realized that I wasn't going to die, I knew I had to decide what to do with the rest of my life.

"I decided, on my own, to come to California. By God I was scared. I was so damned scared that if someone had said 'boo,' I would've jumped ten feet. I didn't know I could do this, but I knew I had to try.

"My brother kept telling me I was crazy. But I reminded him that our grandmother had walked out of Russia, clear across Europe and came to the United States without even knowing the language. She survived. I can at least speak the same language. Why are you telling me I can't do it? What's the worst thing that could happen?

"I've never regretted coming here. It was like coming home."

Exaltation

It's appropriate to follow Sunny's closing comment with the assurance that we may also expect to stand on mountain tops and shout "Eureka," keeping in mind that eventually we'll be moving down from the top and either into a plateau or valley.

I remember feeling tremendous elation, excitement, and the release of great pressure when I chose to move into my own practice.

And there have been other choices for living and balance which have merited equal exaltation: getting in my car and driving westward into an unknown future, marrying Bill, successfully going downhill skiing for the first time, receiving the acceptance call from the publisher.

One can live for days on such mountain tops. The important thing is that we keep alive the memory of such exaltation for those times when, as will inevitably happen, we are struggling with imbalance, a pit or even a pothole.

Guilt

As you move through the process of working/living and unfolding your giftedness, some choices might be turned aside or diminished because we feel guilty about either making them or maybe even just thinking about them.

Like fear, the emotion of guilt covers an attitude which must be examined for its validity in your life. In making choices for the "work" of our lives, men and women alike must respond to an age-old premise: the man must be the provider; the woman must nurture and tend. And now, there's also a contradictory premise which challenges women to seek board rooms and men to change diapers.

Can you see how excessive guilt for *not* obeying either one of these cultural sex-role standards can lead to imbalance? Ever heard these?

Woman: "I graduated top in my field so I guess I'll go on. But I'd really rather stay home and have children."

Man: "I've got to keep this job to put my children through college. That's what fathers are for."

Woman: "I won't be a good mother if I don't prepare a hot, balanced meal every night."

Man: "My wife wants a vacation in Europe. I'd hate to disappoint her."

Woman: "My husband needs me to run the household. He'd never have clean clothes or matched socks if I didn't."

All of these sentiments are fine—*if* you are being

faithful to yourself, *if* you are in balance, *if* you are happy. But if guilt is pushing your choice buttons, it's time to examine just how valid is that sentiment. There is nothing selfish in shifting responsibility, in seeking your own identity, in growing. I've learned that my husband does the wash much better than I, that salads are healthy, and that I don't want a gigantic business practice that takes me away from my family.

On the other hand, I've also observed where guilt has been so exorcised that true damage occurred to others, particularly children. The pursuit for self-growth is not something which takes place in a vacuum. And so it requires careful, honest evaluation to determine if our choices are made with integrity for all parts (and people) in our lives.

The feeling of guilt is not only attached to potential choices for change in sex roles, but it also can influence (if we choose) our balance in other areas of life. The password for letting guilt get the upper hand is "yes."

Case in point: I belong to quite a number of professional organizations, all of which understandably look to members for active participation. Up until last year, I kept nodding yes, sitting on a number of boards, chairing major projects, attending meetings, and trying to wear all the hats of independent consultant, wife, mother, and friend.

My head bobbed up and down like a yo-yo because I felt guilty if I did not actively participate. Underlying that guilt were other attitudes which said, "You will only be a good professional if you accept this work; you will not be liked if you turn down requests for help."

Wow! How's that for putting a real tilt on my working/living? To get back in balance, I have now become very selective in my participation and have learned, in the process, that organizations and members *do* understand.

Knowing when to say "No, thank you" without guilt is a sailing technique which we all could use. It becomes easier the more aware we are of what circles in our lives need reconnection or touching.

Changing Identity—
An Emotional Package

For You

In the process of working and living, as we make choices for movement toward growth and balance, we change—inside and outside. Values and self-perception, even standards of living might alter so that there's a new person staring back at us in the bathroom mirror.

All kinds of emotions present themselves when we look at this unfolding "us": wonder, celebration, delight, bewilderment. Of the many people I interviewed, only those who had yet to claim power and control over their out-of-balance lives viewed themselves with sadness and regret.

⚜

Sean F., the former still photographer-turned-outdoor-video-cameraman, shared his observations about his new identity.

"I know I'm a different person ... gentler, more sensitive, less temperamental. I'm not primarily motivated by making a ton of money, unlike when I was younger. Now that the money is secondary to my enjoyment (living my adventures and experiencing nature), it quite frankly rolls in.

"In the past, for a few years, I earned as much as $10,000 per month. I bought houses, an airplane, fancy cars. Maybe it's okay for people to go through that. But those days are gone and I don't look back. Also at one time, it became an obsession to win awards. It fed my ego and at the time, I had a humongous ego. But that's over.

"I've gone through a real purification and I'm glad I've gone through it now rather than at fifty. Now I can get on with my life. I don't require so much anymore. Little things make me happy."

For Family and Friends

From Sean's story you can readily see how a change in identity, based upon a choice for his "work" influenced many areas of his life. Although he is currently not married, it takes little to imagine what impact his changed identity would have on a wife, family, and friends.

It is well to be aware that changing identity can arouse feelings of insecurity, jealousy, and loss in significant others. It can be the proving ground for marriages and friendships. In fact, dissension over choices for either our "work" or a job might really be rooted in deeper issues. Just read between the lines of the following statement:

"Other women seem to find fulfillment in running a beautiful home and doing charitable work. But not my wife. Instead of appreciating a successful husband who provides for her, she goes on and on about getting a job. My first wife wanted a job and so I gave in. Within one year she had a lover and left me. There's no way I'm going through that again. Someone needs to talk some sense into her."

Get the picture? Not only are there a variety of issues going on here, but it also appears that communication and active listening have been superficial at best.

Now that Richard G. has made the complete transition

from probation officer to playwright, I asked him to tell me how his wife and seven children have managed his new identity and the attendant change in their lifestyle. During the conversation, it became apparent that he and his wife Carol have instilled a collective attitude in their family that influences everything from self-worth to money. It's an attitude which could only come from much open communication and sharing.

❧

Richard G., playwright.

"I know that even if I wasn't going to make money writing, I'd still be a writer because that's what I've discovered I am. I think our kids have that outlook. They know their worth and it's not a dollar bill. They are very self-sufficient and strong-minded about what they want to do with their lives. I kind of think that if we were into material things, they wouldn't have that.

"Carol knows how important this is. She had been after me for a couple of years to make the move. That's why I have a dedication in my book of poetry which says, 'A special thanks to my best friend and wife, Carol, who taught me that a true friend is willing to take a risk for you and will glory in your growth."

"We don't have a budget like a lot of people do because, to us, a budget is very restrictive and says that you can't do what you want to do. Sometimes we get in trouble. Like right now our car has—no kidding—500,000 miles on it! But there are other things which are more important.

"Our kids know we don't have much money and they seem to appreciate what we do have. We're

very close. Sometimes we might not be able to get
the shoes we want because we've done something
else, but we always get by. We're going to survive
even if I didn't earn a penny from substitute
teaching or writing. We would survive, life would to
on. That's our attitude.

"I write in the den with the kids coming in and
playing their records. Sometimes the youngest is on
my lap. That's all right. I don't scrimp my energies
when it's needed in the family.

"When I get afraid or depressed—which isn't
very often—I talk to my wife. I'm not a closed
person, but when I get depressed I do get quiet. And
Carol will say, 'Okay, Richard. Let's talk.' She's
perceptive to my moods and what-have-you."

A change in identity coming from a major work/life
decision can also generate both positive and negative
feelings in friends. In fact, as Richard penned in his poetry
book, perhaps that is the mark of a real friend—someone
who glories in your growth.

*When Carol Z., a single parent and lifelong
educator, left her position as principal to become a
management consultant, she discovered a mixed
reaction.*

"By the age of forty, I reached burnout.
Although I had managed to combine my beloved
arts, dance and music into my work, I had reached a
point of stagnation and overwork. A friend noted
that I was giving 200 percent and it was killing me.
He was right. It wasn't enough to know that I could

go after and get a higher position with the county Department of Education.

"Once I left, the phone started ringing. Comments varied from 'that's great' to 'you're losing your mind.' A number of the principals and administrators expressed concern for my move. I think it was very threatening for them to think about making a change. And so many came up to me and said, 'You know, I wish I could do this.'

"Interestingly, the PTA mothers seemed most traumatized. I had spent hours with these bright wonderful ladies but somehow they saw me as 'leaving them.' I think I was a role model and someone to talk to. I spent much time with a number of them after I made my decision. I think it forced them to focus on their own lives and ask things like: What am I doing? How much of me never gets listened to? What do I want? That latter question was probably the hardest."

Personal Qualities

Throughout the interviews, I became aware that those individuals who were vitally aware of their life's journey, attempting to focus on the "work" of their lives, and consciously choosing paths for balance or temporary imbalance had at least three things in common: a willingness to risk, a high level of self-esteem and confidence, and faith in something or someone outside themselves.

Willingness to Risk

When I was in high school, I memorized the poem *If* by Rudyard Kipling for some speech contest. While so much of it now escapes me, there still remains one line which continues to haunt my subconscious:

"If you could make one heap of all your winnings and risk it on a game of pitch and toss, and *lose,* and start again at your beginnings and never breathe a word about your loss. . . ."

A powerfully strong image burned in my mind the first time I read that line, burned deeper the first time I presented it, and has been branded ever since. What continues to impress me even more than the idea of gambling all you have, is the concept of *joyful* risk. I can imagine no other reason for the absence of moaning, commiseration, and self-flagellation.

I saw this in so many of the people who kindly and courageously shared their personal journeys with me. The riskiest choices for quality living were made because of a deep-felt conviction that this was, in fact, the very thing that *had* to be done. So there was great joy in making the moves.

The willingness to risk contains one other component besides a joyful conviction: an acceptance of the unknown. Sunny F., a lady who has taken more risks than a daredevil, explained it best when she shared the tale of Brilliant Baby, an embryo awaiting birth.

Cuddled within his mother's womb, Brilliant Baby is busily taking notes about his remarkable development. "Oh, boy! Look at my feet. I can wiggle my toes. Aren't I something? Say now, watch me flex my arm muscle. I sure am a strong one. And hair, I've got fuzzy hair!"

In short order, the time had come for Brilliant Baby to

be born. He feels pressure pushing him downward and he despairs. "Oh, no. I'm being forced out of the place. I'll be crushed in the darkness. I'm going to die!"

What a wonderful surprise is obviously in store for the tiny newborn. But without the birthing pressure, our fabled baby would have stayed exactly where he was. Often we do the same. Afraid of what we can't see or understand, we accept less than our full birthright.

There are two other points to consider under the willingness to risk. First, we each have our own perception of what is risky for us. That's a difference which must be accepted and appreciated in each other. What is a risk for me might be a piece of cake for you. Second, the bigger the risk, the bigger the growth.

Mary G., now manicurist.

"I think deciding not to go further in medical school was probably the biggest risk I ever took … the family, future, status, wealth and everything that medicine promises. I'm no longer afraid to risk. If I could live through that, I figure I could probably live through anything. It's the whole idea of quitting once you've started. And I didn't have something else.

"I am who I am. I have no one else to be. I don't have any other script to work from. The only one I know well enough is me. So I can change things about myself, which I do continually. But being somebody else and living up to an image is something I already tried and it didn't work."

Self-Esteem and Confidence

As a complementary attribute to the willingness to risk, growth seekers see themselves as people with possibility. Because they are joyfully eager to risk, their confidence level increases with new experiences. And, I think, many have created small wellsprings to use when their confidence lags.

They are not invincible. Rather, they are willing to accept the outcome of their choices without a loss to their sense of self. As Richard G. said, it didn't matter whether he was paid or not for his writing. All that mattered was that *he knew* it was right for him.

It would appear that individuals who have successfully discovered the "work" of their lives or are busily going about the discovery process, who maintain a rather steady balance, and who eagerly await the next day, have tapped deep into their well of being and found themselves not wanting. Self-esteem and confidence have allowed them to risk, be at odds with the crowd, and grow.

⁂

Such is the case of *Robert H., a former senior acquisitions editor with one of the nation's largest publishing conglomerates.*

He is one of those fortunate individuals who for twenty years has been happily engaged in "work" and not a job, combining his talents with choices for balance. Married fifteen years to Sandy (a registered nurse) with two children, his story demonstrates these qualities as well as a mighty steady hand when it comes to "sailing." ... literally and figuratively.

As his first significant risk, Bob dropped out of

college and engineering hoping to qualify for the Olympics in sailing. Instead, he got drafted.

Second risk: he elected to become a Navy jet pilot.

"As a jet pilot based on a carrier and having seen a number of my buddies die in training, I knew that if I could learn to land a jet on a bobbing carrier and live through it, I could learn to do anything. Actually, I think there are few things I can't do— only those things I haven't tried and therefore I don't know whether or not I can do them."

After the service, a stint selling chemicals in California ended within six months. "I traded the selling of truckloads of chemicals for the selling of textbooks. And I've been in the book publishing business ever since."

Adamant about staying in California rather than returning to the East Coast, he diligently established a track record for solid productivity, using his home as an office.

"I sign a book contract almost every week. I love it. But I must risk. I have complete freedom of choice in selecting my authors and book subjects but I must be willing to live with these choices. Some of my books sold very well and some very poorly. But I'm willing to put my name on both because I'm not afraid to be wrong. By the same token, if every book I signed became a best seller, I wouldn't be signing enough books."

Although during the course of a month, Bob travels around the United States, speaking before groups, teaching, evaluating authors and book projects, attending trade shows, and making personal appearances, he consciously gives priority to the family.

"I enjoy taking Sandy and the kids with me whenever possible, school permitting. I try to bring them all along to our annual company summer meeting in Washington, D.C. It does become expensive but, in the long run, it's worth every penny."

He still prefers to be home with his family, knowing it means taking Robin to flute and art lessons on Wednesdays and Bryan to soccer and guitar lessons on Saturdays. And then, there's also the school car pool which takes his time. But he doesn't mind.

"I love being home. It's a ritual that the children invade my office after school to do their homework. That way I can help them if necessary. Additionally, both Sandy and I take time out to do special things for us: playing bridge, bowling, and sailing.

"I also try and find time for my hobby: Everything wood in this house I made—from the outdoor patio to the kids' bedroom furniture. Even the spa and landscaping were primarily designed and built by me."

With these comments, one can easily see why Bob has continually resisted his company's efforts to relocate him into a more corporate setting. "I have confidence here: teaching, speaking, and publishing. I can do all that plus have time for my family because I reevaluate what I am doing every day. To me, success is doing what you want to do when you want to do it."

Confidence can also be a fickle quality, sometimes hiding when we need it most. I discovered that quite a number of people, including myself, keep a file of what Sunny F. calls TLC (tender loving care) notes. "You put in it all the warm letters, the thank yous, the congratulations. I think our insecurity in life pops up sometimes so that all we see are our lesser qualities. It's healthy to take out that file and remind yourself what you are doing right."

Lastly, confidence and a solid self-esteem permit us to accept new learning curves. Meeting manager Gary R. concludes, "I don't ever want to grow up. I figure that if I'm ever satisfied with where I'm at then I'm not growing anymore. I don't want to stop growing until I'm dead. I want new challenges. If you had asked me two years ago if I could/would do sales, I would've said 'Sorry, that's not my bag.' Now I'm finding out that it's fine."

Faith

Do you recall the story of Marsha, the divorcee who put herself through a masters program and opened her own private school while also raising three sons? When I asked her how she managed that without giving into despair or depression, her answer came as no surprise, "I've always believed in the positive power of God. I know there's a larger force than I which will channel what I need."

The reason I was not surprised by her response is that the majority of people I spoke with all evidenced an awareness of both responsibility to a bigger world and the recognition of a Power beyond themselves. I call this awareness "faith."

I must admit, I hesitate to use the word "faith" because initially it implies an organized structure of beliefs with ritual and symbolic meaning. Rather, in responding to the giftedness of our life and in making choices for living, I see faith more in terms of a relationship. And there are many kinds of relationships with a Being, Force, or Power ranging from a deeply intimate and personal one to a barely nodding acquaintance. Some of us can name who or what we have a relationship with. Others cannot. What matters more is to respond with integrity to whatever relationship we claim.

Although the "spiritual" circle of our life is where we nurture that relationship, faith here also implies a more direct link and influence in our choices for working/living. If the Kingdom of God is within, as I firmly believe, then the process of becoming who we are meant to be is not only faithfulness but downright holiness. And in the process, we are not meant to see through each other but to see each other through.

You've already seen faith at work in some of the other case studies, but I felt a need to share these additional thoughts with you. Although there is a spectrum of faith relationships, it is nevertheless present for all these people.

❧

Cheryl P.:
"I don't have an organized religion, but I do have some inner faith that God is looking out for me. I pray sometimes but often not consciously. I believe in being good to people, in being honest. Yes, I have a faith."

❧

Bill E.:
"I've put together my own spiritually stimulating program because God is important. I even

spent a couple of weekends in an ashram after getting fired. It strengthens your ability to understand anything. You get to God by looking at yourself and the more you look at yourself, the closer you get to God."

❧

Ronda S.:

"Faith in God is important for the celebrating of life. I find it's real important to me to go to church, to set aside that time. It's humbling to realize I am part of a bigger picture. It puts things in perspective. I'm a Methodist—it's a basic brick."

❧

Richard G.:

"We commute over the mountains to a church we've gone to for years. I get my faith from Carol. She's a preacher's daughter. Thanks to her, I've got a second dedication in my poetry book: 'A very special thanks for the love in the world and to the God who provides it.' And he does. We're always taken care of."

❧

Sunny F.:

"I believe that there is a power greater than me and we're all part of it. There's something stronger within us before you get to God. There's a greater us and that greater us is connected to God. I know we can all call upon ourselves to do things we never thought we could do.

"I think I believe in my heart that there are not questions without answers. If we have a question

then the answer is somewhere. We might block the
answer. Nor do I believe there is only one right
answer. I think there are many paths we can take.
None of them are right and none are wrong. They're
just different."

❀

Sandy R.:
"I believe in an Omnipotent Power that makes
sense out of all of this. You must listen to the inner
voice."

❀

Charles D.:
"I have faith in all of us as part of the universe.
My work allows me to do the give-backs to the
world. All you have to do is to pass the baton to one
person, to give one person encouragement. That's
all we have to do to keep this universe going."

❀

For me, I have a hard time separating faith from any
part of my working/living process. And I'm not sure that
within this book I could share the vital impact this relationship has had on accepting and forgiving who I am, on the
opening and closing of doors in my life, on strength that
comes from sources other than my own, on the presence of
so many kinds of love that move like grace, and on faults
and weaknesses that I can only claim as all mine. But this I
do know: it is much easier to traverse mountains and
streams when there's somebody bigger to take your pack or
maybe even carry you across.

Summary

1. Making choices for working/living and balance might be easier if we are prepared for some of the emotions which might help or hinder our sailing.
2. The fear of failure or the fear of success come from negatively viewing the future and responding with feeling-coated attitudes. Some attitudes might be worn out perceptions which do us more harm than good.
3. Some methods for handling fear are:
   - Visualization
   - Jump Right In
   - Worst Case
   - Reality Testing
   - Get Away From It
   - Comedy Capers
   - Worry "Things"
4. Depression results from fear, from unmet expectations, or from loss. The more dramatic the work move, the more probable the loss—particularly if you have developed a significant history with the former place of employment and/or its people.
5. All loss must be mourned by dialogue.
6. You might, and hopefully will, experience exaltation with some "work" choices as well as choices in other areas of life. Keep that memory in a tinderbox for other times.
7. You might experience guilt over a potential change in cultural sex roles. Guilt also throws us out of balance when we can't say "no."

8. A change in work identity might prove the testing ground for marriage, family and friendships.
9. There are three common personal characteristics which appear in individuals who are successfully striving to achieve quality working and living:
    *   Willingness to Risk
    *   Self-Esteem and Confidence
    *   Faith

Food for thought along your voyage:

Be patient to all that is unsolved and love even the difficult question.
— *Rainier Maria Rilke*

Chapter Nine

In Celebration
of Sailing

It is good to have an end to journey towards;
but it is the journey that matters in the end.
—*Ursula K. LeGuin*

Have you ever noticed that frequently the closing chapter of some books reads like a half-time pep talk? Go out and get that goal! Be a success! Win! Be tops!

The emphasis is on achieving an end result.

I guess I'm a little different. I think the victory (and living) is not based upon what you score but rather how you play. Think about it. If you could see your life stretching before you like a road, there would probably be monuments scattered here and there in commemoration of an achieved goal, a success. But between those glittering obelisks lie days of travel—days of your life.

Some of us go through life with our eyes glued on that

monument, letting everything else around us slip by in a peripheral blur. We sit on the uppermost step of our monument, wipe our brow, and proclaim to the world "Yahoo! I've made it. Now I can be happy."

But what about all the time it took to get there? What happened to life in all those days and maybe even years when we were squinting at the distance and running toward some gleaming goal? What if life ended before we got there? Would we then never have achieved what it means to fully live?

Can you see why I feel so strongly that it is the daily sailing, the celebration of our journey, that is in fact the kernel of life?

I am not negating the very real presence of dreams toward which we aspire, goals toward which we aim. We *must* have a vision that keeps us growing, a vision of how we want our life to be and who we want to be in it. And— if we are to be truly free to live—we claim the power to choose to make it happen. The good news is that we don't have to wait until all the pieces come together before we say "Now, this is living."

Hopefully you picked up that feeling in many of the shared stories. People like Cheryl, Robert, Charles, Ronda and others expressed excitement over the fact that their lives were in process, not that they had arrived!

Let me share some other good news. Not only are we powerful people by having the ability to claim what goes into our life, by making choices for growth and balance, by moving through pits, by changing limiting attitudes, but we also have the magic of magnetism.

The Magic Of Magnetism

This is my phrase for the simple tenet: you get back exactly what you put out. Or as Sunny F. phrases it, "Be careful of what you ask for—you might just get it."

While we have all heard that the power of mental imaging can do much with our physical bodies—walking unharmed on burning coals, creating illness, even death—it might come as a revelation to some that we also have the power to influence matters outside our skeletal framework. Specifically, it appears that when we begin to truly uncover the unique "work" which is ours alone to do, the Universe is there to support our effort.

I admit, it does sound all rather mysterious and magical, but I've personally and professionally seen too much to discount that reality. As soon as we begin to do that which energizes us and gives us meaning, a host of seemingly serendipitous people and things come to our aid.

Even when this book was but an untitled mental concept, I began to meet individuals whose stories I kept on file, not really knowing why I was doing it. Once I actively formulated the idea and plunged in, all manner of reference material and resource people suddenly (and I do mean suddenly) appeared. Whatever I needed, when I needed it, was somehow there. I did not plot, plan or belabor this effort.

Do you see the implication? Instead of worrying about reaching the goal of a finished book, it was merely enough to start the journey and to relish each new person and connection that appeared along the road.

I really feel it is so important to share this idea because frequently we have a tendency to say, "Well, those people are different from me so I guess I'll just have to stay

as I am" or, "I can't do this." That's because we think we
have to journey along. But we don't.

Don't take just my most recent experience as a
sample. Let's look at some others.

⚜

When *Steve C.* sold what he had to concentrate
his efforts on his nautical museum and later recon-
struct a period tall ship, *The Californian,* for use as
a training vessel in the state's Youth Sail Training
Program, the magic of magnetism went to work.

"During the building process, maybe even when
we were in the jungles of Belize cutting timber, I
received a call from the Coast Guard historian. It
turned out that the model we were using for our
design was *The Lawrence,* the first Coast Guard
cutter to come to the West Coast. Not only that, but
The Lawrence led directly to the formation of the
Coast Guard Academy.

"That connection gave us needed publicity and
we were named California's official tall ship and the
lead vessel in the Olympic boat parade. When
you're running a non-profit foundation, that
exposure is vital. And thanks to such publicity, the
Sacramento Redevelopment Agency has contracted
with us to build another ship!"

⚜

For *Martin W.,* the commercial artist whose loss
of his business catalyzed renewed efforts in his
beloved wildlife paintings, all it took was a resolution to change geographic locations for balance and
his "work."

"I can't believe it. Everything has fallen into

place. There are fewer jobs in Northern California, but thanks to my wife's former employer, she got a job with a wonderful woman doctor. She's excited about her work. Not only that, but one of the artists has offered me a position in his silkscreening business and we've got homes lined up to rent.

"This was all meant to be. I think I was being tested. Now I can paint not just whales but elk, raccoon and bear. Wildlife is almost like a faith to me. I really become energized by watching people look at my paintings and talk about the animals. Somehow I think they begin to see how we all— humans and animals—fit together. And I hope that the animals do some kind of spiritual talking to the people.

"I'm excited and scared. I'll still keep some commercial accounts in this area and they'll let me work on them even at a distance. That's another unexpected plus. I really do think this was all meant to be."

Charles D. expressed his experience in these terms:

"It's been three years now and something has always worked. Making the commitment, with Providence stepping in, things did break. The free cable show which I started when I made the move now has me doing some video consulting. I've put some productions together and people are paying me. So television has evolved into some income which adds to my other work.

"Everything is coming together. I'm doing a documentary for the college and a documentary on divorce mediation. I'm going to be doing a special for the local medical school on Alzheimer's disease. That's the kind of thing I want to do.

"My strength is coming from my experience. As a counselor, I am what I am selling. I'm being me. I'm doing my part to make it happen and everything is unfolding. One thing is leading to another."

⚜

In the unfolding of *Sunny F.'s* true work as a writer, she recounts numerous events of unplanned assistance.

A casual acquaintance placed the call which sent her scurrying to the university. "A friend tried to get a free truck since I didn't have enough money to move. He ended up renting a truck for $100, moving me to the college, and I never saw him again. And when I came to California, I found that I didn't even have enough to pay the van line. The owner of the hotel where my daughter and I were staying heard about my dilemma and handed me $1,000 in cash— just like that. No note.

"Ever since my experience at the university, I've believed that things are always there when I need them. The job with Disney, my Lockheed connection ... everything has happened at the right time. You get out of life what you put into it. In this terrible, heartless business of script writing, I have met some very wonderful people. I am where I belong."

⚜

The magic of magnetism also works in reverse. An ancient legend tells the story of an evil king who sent his wise servant out to sow oats. But instead of oats, the servant planted wheat and so wheat grew.

The king was furious. He ordered the guards to seize the servant and bring him to the throne.

"Why did you plant wheat, you imbecile? I told you oats," the king thundered.

"Well," replied the servant with his eyes downcast to hide their gleam. "I see you constantly sowing greed, anger, and evil yet expecting good to come to you. So, I naturally followed your wisdom and thought wheat would bring oats."

Now we don't have to be as overt as ye olde shag nasty king to wind up getting exactly what is our due. In fact negativism (my great bugaboo) can also hamper us from really getting the most out of our life. In fact, we can lose the moments.

I did such a thing on this most recent backpacking trip. My husband has a tendency to leave the well-worn trails and head cross country, proclaiming "I can't believe that *someone* hasn't done this before."

The first half of this particular trek was fit for mountain goats and ice-climbing acrobats. I grumbled and groused to myself from then on out. All I could think about was my aching back, the pain in my knees and feet, and the heat. By the end of the eleven-day trip, I was the last one off the mountain—a heap of misery and convinced that I was not cut out for such antics.

Within a few days after our return, when my heat rashes had cleared, the feet felt better, and my back could smile, I started thinking about the trip. Like a flash it occurred to me: Eileen, you did it to yourself!

Although I loved the days in camp, every time I shouldered that pack, I immediately concentrated on everything that was wrong. So I got exactly what I thought about—pain and misery.

What I had neglected to rejoice—yes, rejoice—about, was that I had successfully made it through each day, carrying more weight than I've ever carried, over rougher terrain than I've ever traveled. And the wonderful sights were certainly worth the effort.

Maybe like Martin, it was another lesson I just had to learn.

How often do we all go through our day's sailing with only thoughts about everything that is going wrong? Why not pick out everything that is going right? Or at least congratulate ourselves on the effort? Not only do we reap a self-fulfilling prophesy with negativism, but we've lost a day of living.

Toward a New Way of Thinking— Toward Now

Stand back with me for a minute, and let's look at where we've come. Work has been redefined as that which energizes us, uses our preferred skills, gives us meaning, and from which we draw a sense of self. It is the giftedness which we alone bring into the world but it may or may not be the same as our job.

To truly live, we must become aware of how we are connected and balanced with all areas of our life, in addition to "work." A choice in one area of life carries impact in all and therefore we learn to sail. Whatever direction we head by our mental or verbal expectations, we will—in all probability—get there.

But if it is the sailing which counts most toward

living, then we must become people with a mind-set that shouts "Now!" We must become people of response rather than people of reflex. Response requires conscious behavior; reflex only requires autonomic reaction.

Whether we are, at this very second, shouting from a summit or struggling deep within a ravine, we hold all the resources to respond and truly live. For it is only by soaking in all the gamut of human feeling that we do, in fact, really live. There must indeed be winters in our life if we are ever to have springs.

When arctic blasts move across the mountains, the higher elevations are scoured by gales, burnished by ice, and frozen beneath tons of snow. The miracles born each summer from that onslaught are fragile alpine meadows surrounded by granite cliffs. Here blossoms no bigger than a lentil nestle within the cracks of gray stone, accepting their moment in the sun.

This then is the final triumph of life—finding and living the moments. I'd like to think that the mountain flower's all-too-brief visitation with the sun is what keeps her protected and alive when the world becomes a swirl of cold.

Thus, not only must we celebrate our sailing and the journey itself, but we must also seek out and relish the moments. Corita Kent wrote truthfully when she insisted, "Love the moment and the energy of that moment will spread beyond all boundaries."

For the journeying is made up of moments which, unless we seize them, are gone.

At age forty, Beverly shared with me the wisdom gained from watching her thirty-nine-year-old friend die within a year from cancer.

"I took her with me on a business trip to New York

because she had always loved that bustling city. Heretofore, my method of working was to fly in with just enough time to get to the meetings, do my thing, and then fly home again. Well, I watched her *be* in New York, taking great delight in sights, smells, sounds, and tastes. Seeing her reminded me of how much the city had to offer; how much I lost by only seeing my narrow world.

"Later on, when she was confined to a wheelchair, my husband and I took her to the beach for a picnic. We filled the basket with all her favorite junk food. What a delight! She seized that moment with us, the sand, the surf, the sea gulls, and the crazy food to truly live where she was right then and there.

"She died the next day.

"I now fly to wherever I'm going with an extra day to spare—just to relish where I am. I, a former workaholic, now take one day off in the middle of the work week to be with a friend, to have lunch, to make a moment that is tailored just for my soul. The truth is we must make allowance for the fact that moments are personal treasures."

What "moments" have you most recently experienced? Any today? Whether by chance or by plan, responding to those moments transforms the ordinary into the stellar.

Thank you, fellow travelers, for all the moments which have danced like sparklers in the sharing of this process for our mutual unfolding. I know we have already connected in our journey by mentally supporting each other's deep desire for a quality life and by empowering ourselves to make choices for attaining the "work" of our lives in concert with our total human existence.

Sail on.

Afterword

Just because everything is different doesn't mean anything has changed.
— Irene Peter

In the time since this book first came out some things *are* different. Some are better: Gary R's two-year "trial" business has merged to become a flourishing meeting planning company. George G. has unleashed his creative talents and retired to a city reverberating with art, theater, music, and lower housing prices. Cheryl P. heads public relations for a library system. Joanne T. has a full-fledged kayaking business. More and more companies have become enlightened to the meaning of wellness in the workplace. And Eastern Europe reels with chaos, democracy and confusing capitalism.

Some things are worse: Flattened companies are

asking fewer employees to do more and more. Corporate raiders ride the range and leveraged buy-outs signal uncertainty and turmoil for workers caught in the middle. National childcare policies still get short shrift despite a majority workforce of women. And the cost of the American dream soars to new heights.

Some things just are: Bjorn Borg divorces. Taxes are levied. Hollywood prevails. Seasons continue. And twenty-four hours remains the length of the day. Only twenty-four hours. Perhaps this explains why the search for quality work and life has not changed but intensified. Demands are everywhere and the time which once seemed elastic and obtainable with merely proper "time management" has become elusive. How to work for a living and still be free to live surfaces as the paramount question for all of us.

Now, more than ever, we need to take control over lives that are clearly leading us. We need to step back and relook at our choices, attitudes, and gifts. Transformation is possible, but only if we show up for life, pay attention, tell the truth, and keep a proper perspective. No miracles here but rather a deliberate decision to remain connected to all the five integral parts of our life. To what do we say "yes"? To what do we say "no"? And how do we respond to that choice in a manner that is positive and therefore powerful?

The new list of readings suggest that others are looking for tools and skills to assist us all in coming to grips with the questions. I'm convinced the answers are within.

The journey continues.

Let us sail on.

Recommended Reading

─ ─ ─ ─ ─ ─ ─ ─ ─ ─ ─ ─ ─ ─ ─ ─ ─ ─

Bedrosian, Maggie, *Life Is More Than Your To-Do List,* BCI Press, 1995.

Cameron, Julie, *The Artist's Way,* Jeremy Tarcher, Los Angeles, CA, 1992.

Chopra, Deepok, *The Seven Spiritual Laws of Success,* New World Library, 1994.

Covey, Stephen, *Seven Habits of Highly Effective People,* Simon & Schuster, New York, 1990.

Fields, Rick, et al., *Chop Wood Carry Water,* Jeremy Tarcher, Los Angeles, CA, 1985

Fields, Rick, et al., *As Above So Below,* Jeremy Tarcher, Los Angeles, CA, 1995

Freudenberger, H.J. with Richelson, G., *Burn-out: How to Beat the High Cost of Success,* Doubleday and Company, New York, 1980.

Goleman, Danile, *Emotional Intelligence,* Bantam Books, 1995.

Handly, Robert and Jane, *Getting Unstuck,* Rawson Associates, New York, 1989.

Handly, Robert and Jane, *Why Women Worry,* New York, 1990.

Johnson, Spencer, *The Precious Present,* Doubleday and Company, New York, 1984.

Kabat-Zinn, Jon, *Wherever You Go – There You Are,* Hyperion, 1993.

Lindbergh, A., *A Gift From the Sea,* Vintage, New York, 1965.

Leider, Richard J. and Shapiro, David, *Repacking Your Bags,* Berrett-Koehler, 1995.

McGee-Cooper, Anne, *You Don't Have to Go Home From Work Exhausted,* Bantam, 1992.

Rechtschaffen, Stephan, *Time Shifting,* Doubleday, 1996.

Richards, Dick, *Artful Work,* Berrett-Koehler, 1995.

Rohrlich, Jay B., *Work and Love: The Crucial Balance,* Simon & Schuster, New York, 1980.

St. James, Elaine, *Simplify Your Life,* Hyperion, 1994.

Salsbury, Glenna, *The Art of the Fresh Start,* Health Comm., 1996.

Schor, Juliet, *The Overworked American,* Basic Books, 1991.

Scott, Cynthia, *Take This Job and Love It,* Simon & Schuster, 1988.

Selwyn, Padi, *Living Your Life Outloud,* Pocket Books, 1995.

Sher, Barbara, *Wishcraft – How to Get What You Really Want,* Ballantine, 1985.

Sher, Barbara, *I Could Do Anything If I Only Knew What It Was,* Delecorte, 1995.

Sinetar, Marsha, *Do What You Love and the Money Will Follow,* Dell, New York, 1990.

Treuille, Beverly, *Managing It All,* Master Media, New York, 1988.

Bibliography

Blum, Jeffrey. "Does Money Buy you Happiness?" *Redbook* (October 1983): 79-81, 164.

Callahan, Tom. "Free to Be Bjorn Once More." *Time* (February 7, 1983): 64.

"Expectations in Focus." *Executive Female* (March/April 1984): 16-20.

Freudenberger, H.J., with Richelson, G. *Burn Out: How to Beat the High Cost of Success.* Doubleday and Company, New York, New York, 1980.

Kaiser, Robert Blair. "The Way of the Journal." *Psychology Today* (March 1981), (reprinted from Dialogue House): 64-76.

Kaye, Dr. Beverly. *Up Is Not the Only Way: A Guide for Career Development Practitioners.* Prentice-Hall, New Jersey, 1982.

Kiechell, Walter. "Starting Over." *Fortune* (April 2, 1984): 147-148.

Larsen, J. and Gill, C. *Changing Lifestyles in Silicon Valley.* Cotnos Associates, Los Altos, California., 1983.

Naisbitt, John. *Megatrends.* Warner Books, Inc. New York, New York, 1982.

Pieper, J. *Leisure: The Basis of Culture.* Random House, New York, New York, 1963.

Rohrlich, Jay B. *Work and Love: The Crucial Balance.* Summit Books, Simon & Schuster, Inc., 1980.

Shulgold, Marc. "Parkening Back in Mainstream." *Los Angeles Times* (January 18, 1984): Section VI, 1 and 4.

Terkel, Studs. *Working.* Pantheon Books, New York, New York, 1972.